MOST LIKELY TO SUCCEED:
THE FRAZIER FORMULA FOR SUCCESS®

"GUIDE TO PERSONAL AND PROFESSIONAL ACHIEVEMENT"

EVAN S. FRAZIER

FOREWORD BY FRANCO HARRIS

INFINITE POSSIBILITIES PUBLISHING GROUP, LLC.
FLORIDA

IP Books
Published by Infinite Possibilities Publishing Group, LLC.
email: info@ippublishingonline.com
Website: www.ippublishingonline.com

Cover Design and Layout: Designs by Rachelle www.designsbyrachelle.com

Diagram Illustrator: John Charney

Cover Photograph: Rick Evans

Library of Congress Control Number: 2008921344

ISBN 0-9774243-0-8
      978-0-9774243-0-6

Printed in the United States of America

First Edition: February 2008
10 9 8 7 6 5 4 3 2 1

"I have known Evan Frazier for more than ten years and have always admired him as a leader and visionary. Evan has spoken on our campus on numerous occasions. His Frazier Formula for Success concept has been well received by students, faculty, and alumni."
                                                    -JARED COHON, PH.D.,
                                        PRESIDENT, CARNEGIE MELLON UNIVERSITY

"Most Likely to Succeed embodies the principles that have made Evan Frazier an inspiration to so many people over the years. Applying the Frazier Formula to your life can truly help you capture and achieve your dreams."
                                                    -JEFF BROADHURST
                                        PRESIDENT, EAT'N PARK RESTAURANTS

"Most Likely To Succeed by Evan Frazier is a must read. Several years ago when I first learned about 'The Frazier Formula For Success' concept, I was impressed and immediately shared it with my leadership team."
                                                    - RICK JOHNSON
                        CHIEF FINANCIAL OFFICER, PNC FINANCIAL SERVICES GROUP

"Reading Most Likely To Succeed and learning about The Frazier Formula For Success are powerful ways to better yourself and to inspire and motivate your team to a higher level of performance. As a part of our professional development program, I invited Evan Frazier to speak and share his Frazier Formula seminar with our African American managers at Enterprise. The response was overwhelmingly positive and many of our managers ended up taking on new leadership roles and being clearer about their career direction with us."
                                                    - TIM NETTLES
                VICE PRESIDENT/GENERAL MANAGER, ENTERPRISE RENT-A-CAR

"The Frazier Formula provides information that can inspire individuals to achieve and want more out of life. I've seen it inspire high school students, college students, and young professionals. It even inspired me to go to graduate school and get my MBA."

-KELLY L. RUSSELL, MBA
PROGRAM ADMINISTRATOR
CITY OF PITTSBURGH-PITTSBURGH PARTNERSHIP

"Evan and The Frazier Formula helped me to stay focused on completing my barber's license and inspired me to start a commercial cleaning business that has been growing."

- MARVIN PRENTICE, JR.
LICENSED BARBER AND ENTREPRENEUR

"Mr. Frazier is a genius when it comes to the art of success. He has changed my perspective on life in and outside of the boxing ring. He possesses the winning formula to turn anything you touch into gold!"

- TIKA HEMMINGWAY
USA BOXING NATIONAL CHAMPION & COLLEGE STUDENT

"For those of us who teach public affairs, the notion that professionals can successfully cross the blurred borders of the public and private sectors during a career is an important idea. My approach is simply to have Evan share his journey and his 'Formula' with my students. To them, and to me, he is a 'rock star'."

- BOB STUMPP, ADJUNCT FACULTY
UNIVERSITY OF PITTSBURGH, GRADUATE SCHOOL OF PUBLIC AND
INTERNATIONAL AFFAIRS

DEDICATION

To my wife Holly, you are the love of my life, a wonderful mother, and an extraordinary example. You have a highly demanding professional career, yet you never allow your position to overshadow your priority for family.

To my oldest son Evan Jr., you are destined for greatness, as I already see signs of a scholar-athlete emerging within you.

To my daughter Nia, a talented dancer and drama queen, the sky is the limit as you excel in school and pursue the passion that you have for the arts.

To my youngest son William, you say the best prayers and have a smile that lights up the whole room. Your greatness lies in simply being who you are, trusting God, and following your dreams.

Most Likely To Succeed is dedicated to my whole family. I love you all very much. Thank you for keeping me grounded and putting up with the long hours that my career and civic pursuits demand. I hope that the principles in this book will serve as a guide for your future success!

ACKNOWLEDGEMENTS

First, I am grateful to God for guiding me through this process of writing *Most Likely to Succeed: The Frazier Formula for Success* in His time and not my own. While He gave me a vision for the completed project years ago, He had a tendency to direct this project in stages and to not let me get ahead of myself.

Mr. Franco Harris is truly an inspiration both on and off the field. A very special thanks goes out to Mr. Harris for his generous contribution in writing the Foreword for "Most Likely to Succeed." I am deeply honored and humbled to have his support and involvement in this way.

Dr. Keshia Abraham, an exceptionally talented writer who became my primary editor and book consultant. I am eternally grateful for her willingness to assist me in ensuring my voice came across clearly in my writing.

Thanks to Shelley Parris Williams and Infinite Possibilities Publishing Group for their interest, expertise, and guidance in completing my first book.

Mr. John Charney, a talented and compassionate administrator at Winchester Thurston School, who drafted the diagrams featured throughout the book.

Mr. Steve Irwin, Esq. for his personal support over the years and for the legal guidance provided by his law firm Leech Tishman Fuscaldo and Lampl.

Ms. Betsy Fitzpatrick, a phenomenal writer, who provided assistance in helping to complete a key section of this book and for encouragement over the years on this project.

Thanks to the following individuals for their assistance in reviewing my manuscript. They include: Cynthia Pearson Turich, Terri Baltimore, Tris Ozark, Laura Kornegay, Rachel Blakey, and my wife Holly Hatcher-Frazier.

Mr. Thomas Buell, Jr., Dr. Audrey Murrell, and Ms. Deesha

Philyaw, each are talented writers who made important contributions to this project over the years.

Special thanks to Dr. Kenneth Blanchard, Co-author of "The One Minute Manager" series, for providing inspiration and feedback along the way.

A very special thanks to all of those individuals who assisted me in better understanding the writing and publishing process: Linda Dickerson, Judy A. Kelly, Cheryl Towers, LaMont Jones, Charles Walker, and Dr. Lawana Gladney.

Thanks also to Bill Buck, Esq., Edwin Jackson, and Nina Lynch for their support.

A special thanks to Jeff Broadhurst, Jana Sharlow, Eat'n Park Restaurants, and the entire Broadhurst Family, for supporting my book pre-launch at the 2008 National Society of Minorities in Hospitality Conference. Their commitment to the book provided the motivation and encouragement needed to complete this project.

There are many people who supported me in this project over the past ten years:

Rev. Dr. Mary Buckley from Mt. Ararat Baptist Church, who confirmed for me that my work had potential. I recall her saying "The ideas are not dead, they are definitely alive."

Dr. Cynthia Mayo, director of the hospitality program at Delaware State University and was also the Co-Publisher of a CHRIE publication, who gave me my first opportunity to share The Frazier Formula for Success® with an international audience.

Thanks to special advisors Dr. Ernest Boger (University of Maryland Eastern Shore), Dr. David Corsun (University of Denver), Dr. Beverly Bryant (North Carolina Central University), Ron Davenport, Jr. (Sheridan Broadcasting), and my brother Andrew Frazier, Jr. (Executive Leadership Council).

Thanks to Ms. Esther Bush and the Urban League of Greater Pittsburgh for the opportunity to share my concepts with Urban League audiences, both local and national.

Special Recognition to my cousin Gemal Woods (Park Triangle Productions), an exceptionally talented filmmaker in Washington D.C. who made it possible to have a high quality Frazier Formula DVD to accompany my seminars.

Mr. Bob Brevard, a truly world-class graphic designer who helped to create The Frazier Formula for Success® brand.

Ms. Kezia Ellison, who helped tailor The Frazier Formula for Success® towards youth.

Thanks goes out to Mike Jasper, who helped me to develop a business plan/investment proposal for the project and Alan Isaacs, a talented career coach who provided solid assistance along the way.

Thanks to the entire National Society of Minorities in Hospitality members, chapters and national board for your inspiration and support on this project.

Completing this book could not have been done without the support of Greg Spencer and the Hill House Association Board, Mel Steals, Jr. and the Hill House Economic Development Corporation Board, support of the Hill House executive team, my executive assistant, and the inspiration of the hundred plus Hill House employees.

Thanks to my network of mentors for your support in keeping me lifted up at all times.

Thanks to family members: Andrew and Brenda Frazier, William and Gwendolyn Hatcher, Heather Hatcher, Warner and Janine Macklin, Andrew Jr. and Janae Frazier, Saryn and Michelle Hatcher, my wife Holly and kids, my extended family and many others.

Thank you to all,
Evan S. Frazier

TABLE OF CONTENTS

Conclusion

Bibliography

FOREWORD

Sometimes situations we face in life may seem impossible. Just like the day of December 23, 1972, when my team, the Pittsburgh Steelers, were playing the Oakland Raiders in the divisional playoff game. We were winning the game with less than two minutes to go. As rarely happened, our defense got out of position and the Raiders' Kenny Stabler ran more than 30 yards for a touchdown, a remarkable play in itself, to give the Raiders a 7-6 lead with just over a minute to play.

We were stunned – we were so close to winning the first playoff game ever in Steelers history, and it had just slipped away. We stood in silence. We stood in disbelief. After the ensuing kickoff, it all came down to one play: 4th down, 22 seconds on the game clock, no time outs, and 62 yards to the end zone.

In every play there is an opportunity. The play called for this 4th down was 66 Circle Option, which required me to stay in the backfield and block. But when the quarterback, Terry Bradshaw, had to scramble out of the pocket, I decided to run downfield as a pass receiver. What happened next passed by in an instant, yet has lived on as one of the most celebrated plays in NFL history. As I was headed downfield Bradshaw threw the ball to Frenchy Fuqua and there was a collision. In a split second the ball was on its way to me. And then I was on my way to the end zone. And the Steelers were on their way to their first ever playoff victory. The play was named "The Immaculate Reception," born out of a seemingly hopeless situation.

Every week in football we had a game plan. This preparation was essential if we wanted to win. The plan was not guaranteed to work perfectly, but we practiced like it would – every time I touched the ball I ran to the end zone. Touchdown. This mental and physical preparation showed me where I wanted to go and made me aware of obstacles I would face – and how to overcome them.

Not everyone plays football or has a game plan handed to them. But now you have a chance to have your own game plan handed to you by reading *Most Likely To Succeed: The Frazier Formula for Success*. Success on and off the field is more about making something out of the circumstances that arise than about knowing exactly what is going to happen ahead of time. You need to adapt to the situation at hand.

Every day will not be miraculous, but every day there is an opportunity somewhere to succeed. Will you be ready?

Take *The Frazier Formula for Success* and prepare for life's many opportunities as well as its inevitable challenges. If you consistently apply this formula, you too will see the opportunities in a deflected pass. Keep your mind sharp, your eyes open, and your hands ready, and you will be amazed at what you can do when the opportunity comes for you to succeed. Catch it and run with it: *The Frazier Formula for Success*.

- Franco Harris
Superbowl MVP & NFL Hall of Famer

PREFACE

My purpose in writing "Most Likely to Succeed" is to share with you a success framework that I have used in my own life and one that has helped others to find and achieve success in their lives. In fact, sharing this book with you is a part of my own personal vision for success. For as long as I can remember, a major way that I define success in my own life includes having a positive impact in the lives of others. I believe that since God has blessed me in countless ways, it is my responsibility to be a blessing to others.

This book is very special to me for a lot of reasons. Initially when I first started thinking about titles for this book, my thoughts went back to experiences I had in high school and college when students were given special titles that seemed to define them in some way. I'm sure you are familiar with these sometimes serious and sometimes humorous titles like "Best Dressed," "Most Talkative," "Most Popular," and other such monikers. Personally, I never paid a whole lot of attention to these titles but in high school and college groups, I always found myself being selected for the title "Most Likely to Succeed." While I never sought it out, this seems to be the way people have viewed me throughout my life.

Early on, I was put in positions that carried great responsibility, and required teamwork, vision, and understanding. At the age of eight, my older brother Andrew and I started a paper route business. We delivered papers seven days a week for six years straight. During this time I remember playing on baseball and football teams, and participating in my school district's Gifted program one day a week. Toward the end of elementary school, I remember serving as class president and as the captain of the safety patrol.

It was during this time that my mother, Brenda Frazier, was very involved in the women's movement and in civic affairs. I remember traveling with her throughout the country as she participated in conventions and marches. Traveling with my mother, I met numerous congressmen, senators, and other national personalities who were influential and inspired me. It was during these years that I also became heavily involved in my church. I still have clear recollections of being an overwhelmed fifth grader who believed so seriously that if I worked really hard and continued to prepare myself, I could become President of the United States, I even convinced my parents.

In middle school, I continued to stay active in academics, sports, and building my paper route business. I also became involved in Student Council and by the time I was in eighth grade had become its president. As I moved into high school, I was already thinking about colleges and became very interested in business. While I took challenging academic courses, my focus was not solely on school work. I worked hard to find experiences that would prepare me in business to be successful in life. I ended up participating in Junior Achievement (a program that taught youth about entrepreneurship and business) for four years and became quite active in competitions, conferences, and in taking on leadership roles. Other experiences in high school included participating in Presidential Classroom (a program in Washington DC to teach students about government), traveling to Italy for three weeks through a

Rotary International exchange program, and earning a black belt in karate.

One of the defining experiences during my teenage years came through attending one of the Junior Achievement conferences, where I met James Broadhurst, Chairman and CEO of Eat'n Park Restaurants. After I participated in one of his seminars on business ethics, he approached me and started a conversation that became pivotal for me. This conversation led to an opportunity to learn about the restaurant business while I was in high school; it facilitated future college scholarships; and, it helped create the opportunity to attend Cornell University's School of Hotel Administration. While at the time my thinking was simply focused on attending college to study business administration, the opportunity to learn about hospitality management from a world-renowned institution was unique, and I didn't feel that it would compromise my ability to gain a broader business education.

My undergraduate career mirrored my previous educational experiences. Although academics were very important to me, they were not my sole focus. Once again, I took on a variety of leadership roles ranging from president of the Minority Business Student Association to co-founder of the National Society of Minorities in Hospitality, and a host of other extracurricular activities and work experiences. However, there were certain subject areas such as organizational theory and management, where I had the opportunity to go much deeper as a teaching and research assistant.

When I was a college senior, I was trying to find something meaningful to write about in the yearbook. In the process of reflecting on my experiences and successes, I found myself also thinking about other students on campus who clearly stood out as people who were going to really make it in this world. A funny thing that I observed was that the individuals who stood out as "Most Likely to Succeed," at least in my mind, were not always at the top of their class. In fact, there were three characteristics that I found in common with those individuals. When I started to reflect on these common characteristics, I realized that they were similar to how I always tended to think about achieving my own goals. Most students on campus had one or two of the characteristics developed pretty well; however, it was those individuals who had all three who clearly stood out as having a significant advantage. Therefore, I simply wrote in Cornell's "Ethos Yearbook":

"The three ingredients to success include:
a Vision, a Plan, and the Right Attitude!!"

Over time, I found that these three common characteristics have universal application and appeal. Over the past fifteen years, I have had the opportunity to share and expand upon this concept so often that I'm convinced that it has impact in helping people tap into their success. As I speak to high school, college, or professional audiences, I continue to be met with a very positive response. I often hear people indicate that they were inspired to go back to school, dream bigger, focus in on a career path, pay more attention to personal matters, and to be more deliberate and focused about how they approach their future. This concept has manifested itself into articles that I've written, PowerPoint presentations, a DVD teaching tool, and a formalized seminar known as **The Frazier Formula for**

Success®. It is my intention to share this powerful concept with you in hope that you will apply it to your life and share it with others.

UNIT I

Introducing the Frazier Formula for Success

CHAPTER 1

YOUR GUIDE TO SUCCESS

Understanding "The Frazier Formula"

Success is something that we each desire and define in different ways. For some people, success is viewed strictly in terms of material prosperity. By their definition, being successful might mean attending a prestigious school, attaining their dream job or position, or perhaps embodying a certain status in society. It might even mean having a certain lifestyle including a beautiful home, a fancy car, and lots of financial reserves. For others, success might come from a sense of personal and/or moral prosperity including living a principled life, raising a family, contributing to their community, or being true to a certain spiritual faith. And for many of us, it might involve a combination of different forms of prosperity while maintaining a principled life that is balanced, and ensuring a life that genuinely makes us feel good.

Initially, thinking about success can be confusing. First, you have competing definitions as to what success means or should mean. Then, you have competing interests from individuals and institutions that seek to define success for you. From as early as elementary school, your family, friends and society at large have a way of influencing how you define success. Ultimately, you wonder how to make life and career decisions that will help you to be most complete and successful.

The formal definition of "success" according to Webster's Dictionary, is "a favorable or satisfactory outcome or result."

With this understanding, Most Likely to Succeed will help you expand the Webster Dictionary definition by not only helping you define success for yourself, but also helping you plan for success by linking other important elements to help you better achieve your goals by creating more "favorable outcome(s) or satisfactory result(s)."

This book is divided into two main sections. In the first part, Unit I, The Frazier Formula for Success is outlined in detail beginning with an introduction to the main concepts. This introductory chapter will provide a framework for how you can apply The Frazier Formula for Success to your life. Each of the remaining chapters in Unit I will explain in greater detail how this formula can be used as a tool to help you be more successful on your personal and professional journey. Unit II builds on the knowledge gained in Unit I, showing the lessons of The Frazier Formula at work. This second section builds on stories from a range of people who have lead inspirational lives.

The Frazier Formula for Success (or simply "The Frazier Formula") is designed to serve as a broad framework for you to better understand success. It is intended to help you build a roadmap that will guide you in reaching your goals and to give you a perspective that will help you achieve both personal and professional success in your life. And the best thing about it is that no matter what your circumstance in life might be, it can apply to you.

If you are a student, The Frazier Formula can help you think long term about your life and career aspirations and allow you to develop a plan that maximizes your options based on your personal interests. From helping you think strategically about your academic major and the type of classes that you should consider, to encouraging the types of activities that can help you reach your goals, the Frazier Formula will help you build a career and life plan that incorporates your personal and professional interests.

If you are a working professional, The Frazier Formula can help you reflect on your successes while working with you to clarify those missing elements of what it is that you ultimately want to achieve. It will help you to think strategically about different options that you encounter and to ensure that you build a plan and make decisions that are clearly aligned to your personal Vision. It will also help you to see beyond just the professional and establish balance through additional focus on the personal elements.

If you are unemployed, underemployed, or looking to change careers, the best way to find new opportunities is to be clear about where you want to go and consider the value that you can bring to the world or to a specific role. This is where The Frazier Formula can make an impact.

If you are an individual who has a lot of potential but who has no idea how or where to direct your talent and perhaps you still don't know what you want to be when you grow up, The Frazier Formula can work with you to clarify your thinking and assist you in finding more satisfaction in your career plans and life decisions.

The bottom line is that no matter what your circumstance might be, The Frazier Formula can help you to better yourself and become successful as long as you take the time to apply its principles appropriately. While no book can guarantee you success just from reading it, reading this book will help you to equip yourself to be "most likely to succeed." It will also help you to understand that both personal and professional considerations are important to examine. Practicing The Frazier Formula has proven that both personal and professional goals are important in the quest for success. Once you read *Most Likely to Succeed: The Frazier Formula for Success*, your success will rest on your ability to apply its components to your own life.

The Frazier Formula for Success can be described in many ways. Some prefer to think about it as an equation:

$$S = V\,P\,A^r$$

This stands for Success equals Vision x A Plan x The Right Attitude. Technically speaking, if you were to examine this equation literally, you would find that ideally the S (Success) should be the highest number possible. Therefore, since Vision, A Plan, and The Right Attitude are multiplied by each other, each greatly affects the total outcome. It would also be important to note that the r ("right" attitude instead of "wrong" attitude) will have an exponential impact on the other numbers. This signifies that a really positive or right attitude that is in alignment with your Vision will take you much farther than any other individual component. It also signifies that if any of the three components is out of alignment, it affects the total success outcome and therefore, the three components of The Frazier Formula are inextricably linked.

Others prefer to think about the Frazier Formula in a listed format:

Success =
1. Vision
2. A Plan
3. The Right Attitude

In general, Vision is your future outlook for what you seek to achieve. A Plan is essentially a roadmap that has specific tangible goals that you need to accomplish as you journey toward your Vision. And The Right Attitude represents your personal outlook or perspective that should be in alignment with your Vision. While each component taken by itself is important, it is the collective alignment and synergy among the three that gives you the exponential advantage.

One of the unique aspects about the Frazier Formula for Success is that it is very easy to remember. It has only three key components to memorize as opposed to seven, ten, or twelve. I will never forget attending a National Society of Minorities in Hospitality conference about a dozen years ago. A young lady walked up to me to introduce herself. As I tried to introduce myself back to her she quickly replied, "I know who you are. You spoke to us last year. You told us about The Frazier Formula for Success: vision, a plan, and the right attitude." I looked at her in amazement. I could hardly believe that after a year she remembered all three parts of the Frazier Formula from a seven- to ten-minute speech. That experience prompted me to think about how I could share this unique and powerful framework in a more formalized way. *(See diagram A-1)*

When you think about the components of the Frazier Formula: Vision, A Plan, and The Right Attitude, it is important that they are in alignment with each other. If you develop a plan for your life and career that is not based upon your ultimate vision, then there is an inherent flaw in your approach. Imagine that your goal in life was to be a Supreme Court Justice; however, the plan that you built for yourself included graduate

The Frazier Formula for Success ®

The Model

Vision

S

A Plan

The Right
Attitude

A-1

school but not law school. I'm sure that you would agree that the logic in this scenario was dysfunctional at best, since you must first be a lawyer to be qualified as a judge, let alone a Supreme Court Justice.

Perhaps you want to teach at the university level and part of your plan is to secure a doctorate degree. However, you are the type of person that not only does not like research but, in the face of adversity, you have a tendency to quickly give up. First there is a need to clarify your vision and the type of opportunities that most interested you within academia. You will first want to examine why you want to be a professor and what kind of role you realistically want to pursue. Second, completing a doctorate degree takes years and requires significant perseverance. Therefore, your vision to become a university professor can be achieved; however, you will need to take into consideration the type of school that you plan to target, your motivations for that specific career direction, and what kind of attitude you will need to help you endure the lengthy academic preparatory journey that you will need to take.

Let's say that your professional goal is to become a general manager of a hotel or restaurant. First, you will need to think through which aspect of the hospitality industry best aligns with your vision and why. You will need to think about lifestyle and other personal considerations such as how much traveling you are willing to endure and how often you are willing to move to different cities or even countries. As you make important career decisions and build your plan, you will need to take into account your personal and professional interests. In addition, adopting a hands-on approach and service-oriented attitude in this industry will help you to be most successful. You will need an attitude that allows you to interact effectively with customers, employees, and contractors in a way that allows you to maximize your operation. Using the Frazier Formula as a success framework can help you become "most likely to succeed" in this industry or any other.

Some people have a hard time aligning their vision with their plan because they have conflicting views of success. On the one hand, they continue to maintain a career that makes them seem successful, but at the same time, they feel unsatisfied in this career. Unfortunately, without their own definition of success, these people remain potentially unfulfilled.

As you continue your journey through reading *Most Likely to Succeed*, you will be given more detail as well as examples about the Frazier Formula For Success along the way. This success framework can help you to develop new or refine existing personal and professional goals. Unit I will clearly give you a solid understanding of the Frazier Formula and Unit II will complement Unit I, making sure the key and subtle points do not get overlooked.

In an effort to use *Most Likely to Succeed* as a tool for your life, I recommend that you use one of two approaches. Either read through the entire book, and then come back to Unit I and re-read chapters 2, 3, and 4 on separate days. You can start using these chapters to help you develop your vision, build your plan, and align your attitude with your vision. After you have started to commit your Vision, Plan, and Attitude characteristics to paper, then re-read Unit II. For those individuals who are unlikely to go back after they finish reading a book, my recommendation is to read chapters 1 and 2 and then take a pause to start writing your own vision statement. On a separate day, read chapter 3 again, pausing to start building your plan. Repeat this same process for Chapter 4 on a separate day. Then once you have gone through this process, read all the chapters in Unit II at your own pace as you will already be able to relate them to your own experiences. Regardless of the approach that you decide to use, the important factor is to internalize the material so that you can effectively apply the Frazier Formula model to your life.

It is expected that most people working with the Frazier Formula will claim this opportunity to fine tune and clarify some aspect of their vision, to review the plans that develop to achieve this vision and to adjust aspects of attitude to become more productive. However, as you can see from diagram A-1, there needs to be clear alignment between the components to achieve success.

Ultimately, using the Frazier Formula as a tool will help you to think more strategically about how you can optimize your success. This book and the Frazier Formula framework will also apply to those individuals who may not be as driven professionally or those who find themselves much more interested in personal achievements outside of the workplace. And keep in mind, you do not have to be Ivy League educated to apply this model to your life. The Frazier Formula can apply to everyone.

There is also a connection between the personal and professional aspects of your life that will be explored in this book. Regardless of the type of career you pursue, certain personal behaviors will clearly affect your ability to be successful, either positively or negatively. It is important to understand that living your personal life in a way that includes substance abuse or other destructive behaviors can have a negative impact on your success. It can not only hamper your ability to achieve success but, in other cases, it can limit your ability to sustain the successes that you have already achieved. The Frazier Formula will give you tools to help you clarify and evaluate the types of goals that you will need to establish in both your personal and professional life as you strive to achieve your ultimate vision.

The upcoming chapters in Unit I will give you more details about each of the Frazier Formula components and share examples to better illustrate how you can apply them to your life. Chapter 2 will give you a clear understanding of Vision and how you can establish a clear vision in your life. Chapter 3 outlines the technical and strategic components of how you can build your plan through practical steps that lead to vision fulfillment. Chapter 4 will demonstrate how you can align your attitude with vision in a way that allows you to maximize your potential.

Every good book or powerful concept starts with a basic core idea. Reading Unit I will help you to understand a simple, yet powerful framework – The Frazier Formula For Success® – that you can immediately apply to your life. Your understanding of this success framework will not only add to your knowledge, it will fundamentally change your outlook and enhance the way you prepare for your future.

CHAPTER 2

CREATING A VISION

DEFINING YOUR GOALS

The concept of vision is ultimately simple, yet it can have a most profound impact on the major life decisions that you make. The Frazier Formula for Success starts with Vision, because it is a very powerful tool and an essential component in defining success on your own terms. Vision is your future outlook or aspiration for what you eventually want to achieve in life. It could be a twenty year outlook or a life long journey. The great thing about it is that there is no right or wrong answer. The character and nature of your Vision will frame the types of things that you pay attention to and it will impact your decision-making throughout your life. The Vision serves as your strategic guide, and it serves as a tool to check in with yourself periodically. Think of it as your self-determined measure of success.

Having a Vision Statement is very personal and it should reveal some of your core values. If you are not motivated by your own personal Vision, then essentially it is useless. This picture of success that you paint in your head flows from something that comes from deep down inside of you. It reflects the way you are made, your personal DNA, and the things that matter the most to you. When you think about your Vision, imagine you have a blank canvas on which to create your own images. A concept discussed by Steven Covey in *The Seven Habits of Highly Effective People* is also extremely useful to keep in mind. Among his recommendations for healthy habits to develop, he suggests beginning with the end in mind so that your destination is clear.

The vision that you set for yourself will partially determine major life decisions that you make. It is extremely important to understand how powerful a person's vision can be in the development and success of their professional career. Individuals who have clear purpose and direction are more grounded, and therefore often more successful, because they know where they are headed. People grounded in this way are not as concerned about politics in the organizational environment, or about compromising their integrity, because they always have alternative choices they can make to stay on track. Once you have established a vision, you have something you can call to mind any time life threatens to take you off track.

Vision is what helps you keep your "eyes on the prize" and it keeps the focus where it needs to be while giving you a tremendous advantage over your competition. While I do believe that everyone has vision to some degree, there is a great difference between those who have a clear vision and those who continue to have a changing or fuzzy vision. For many people, their vision of what they want to achieve in life is not clear at all. In fact, in the absence of their own well-thought out vision, many people adopt society's vision for success. This might include falling prey to pop culture's definition of success, your company's philosophy of success for your life, or perhaps allowing those individuals that you are around most frequently to shape your definition of success. This can be contrasted with being clear about your vision and selecting the companies, friends, and associates that complement your personal vision.

Even though there is no wrong answer when it comes to Vision, if you are not an active participant in shaping your Vision, it is likely that your commitment level to achieving that Vision is less than what it could be. You can often tell the difference between someone who is focused on their vision and someone who is just going through the motions. When you see someone who has a focused vision, the difference in their confidence level and clarity is noticeable. You might even notice that these are the people who can inspire you without even doing anything – it's simply their presence and sense of clarity that shines through enough to prompt you to call to mind your own vision.

As you create your Vision, remember that it is yours and yours alone. This is something that you should definitely decide by yourself; otherwise, you run the risk of allowing someone else to define your life and who you should be. Please realize that this does not mean you cannot have discussions with other people. It means that you should not allow anyone to have a final say about your Vision. It is your Vision and you will be the one who will live with it and be motivated by it. Protect

your vision and care for it like you would take care of
something or someone extremely precious and valuable to you.

THE VISION STATEMENT

One of the best ways for people to have clarity in their
vision is to create a 'Vision Statement' for themselves. You can
start crafting a vision statement by simply taking the time to
document the vision that you have in your head. There are
many ways this can be done; you might choose to write it out,
describing your vision in detail, or perhaps you might draw or
paint it. Another effective way of crafting your vision statement
is to gather images that reflect your personal vision and use the
images to help you to write. Once you have it committed to
paper, take the time to refine it until you are able to actively
reflect the picture of success that you painted in your mind.
And from here, you are empowered with the ability to alter your
vision, making it real and motivational to you.

The purpose of writing your vision statement and
committing it to paper is to help solidify and formalize your
vision in your own mind. There is no specific format that a
vision statement must take; however, there are some general
guidelines to keep in mind. Your vision statement can be as
specific or general as you need it to be. In addition, it can focus

on achieving something specific, imagining a general lifestyle that you want to attain, or developing a philosophy or discipline that you desire to uphold. Your vision statement might even be about the type of impact you want to make on the world. Typically, the more succinct, specific, and detailed you can be the better, as this makes it easier to envision, articulate, and use your vision as a foundation for establishing specific goals and determining steps to achieve it.

There is something psychological that takes places when a person takes time to commit to their dreams or aspirations by writing them down. It is the difference between something becoming real or just remaining a fleeting thought. Once you see it in front of you it gets concretized. There is documented proof that writing it down actually helps people to commit to their ideas thereby translating dreams and ideas into something real and tangible. Taking the time to really think about, craft, and commit to your vision will make it much easier to see the road ahead.

So the question then becomes, if Vision Statements are so important and powerful, why don't more people have them? The problem for most people is not having a faulty vision statement; it is not having a defined vision statement at all. And it is not that people do not have the ability to create their own vision. One reason that most people don't have a vision statement is because they are afraid to commit to any kind of a long range goal. For some people, it is simply something they never realized they needed to think about. And for others, the idea of long range planning feels too challenging when dealing with their immediate circumstances. Also, to summarize your life in a single statement or sentence can be frightening. Ultimately, the greatest fear is, "What happens if I don't reach my goal? Will I then be a failure?" The answer is *NO! You are not a failure!* It is just human nature to want to avoid failure at all costs and to want to keep ourselves from being in a position that we feel holds us accountable for achieving our personal goals.

It is important to understand that establishing a clear vision is designed to be directional. It does not have to be absolute. In other words, if you did not achieve your vision to become President of the United States, but you became a high ranking official and powerful force at the national level, then your vision helped to provide an important strategic direction in your life. I know of a gentleman whose vision was to become the U.S. Secretary of State. Although he never achieved this position, he did become the head of a major national foundation, and as he reflected on his life, he was very content with his accomplishments. Had it not been for his vision to become Secretary of State, he might not have taken the steps that helped him to be in a position to run such a prestigious foundation that has worldwide impact.

Another reason that people are resistant to creating a vision statement is because they really don't know specifically what they want to be when they grow up. And that's fine. Many times during our developmental education, it is demanded of us that we be able to say what it is that we want to be, but how often are we really presented with the tools or skills to really take this question to heart and make it individually meaningful?

Creating a vision statement removes the pressure from the outside and gives you the room to be as general or as specific as you need to be for your own sake. You might even feel driven to create statements that reflect each aspect of your life individually. This might mean creating a statement for your career or professional life, one for your relationships with other people, one that involves family, and/or one that highlights hobbies and personal interests that you want to cultivate. It is then important to step back and try to balance these aspects with what's ultimately most important to you. Your vision statement becomes more strategic when you think through key questions and are able to be clear about incorporating the things most important to you in the proper way. Are your personal interests driving the professional? Are your professional interests driving your personal agenda, or perhaps it's about lifestyle or impact for you. Do these subtle but important differences come across clearly in your vision statement? What are the core drivers behind what is most important to you? Your personal vision statement should reflect where you think you might want to be using language that mirrors your vision. Diagram A-2 gives you some different ways to think about crafting a vision statement that goes beyond a singular or specific professional accomplishment.

The Frazier Formula for Success ®

Vision

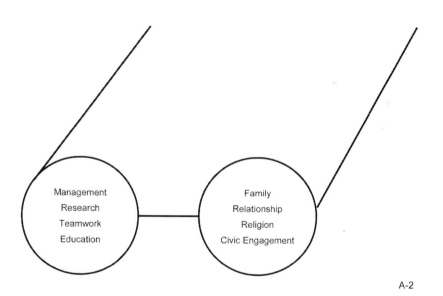

A-2

I notice that often people have the tendency to think about educational milestones as a part of their vision. Think about it, how often have you heard someone say, "my ultimate goal or vision it to graduate from college," "obtain my law degree," or "graduate from medical school"? I encourage you to develop a vision that delves beyond these educational goals and ask yourself, "What is it that you want to achieve with your education"? The danger in having your educational goals in your vision is that it leaves a void once you achieve this educational milestone. It would leave your vision to be somewhat myopic and less strategic if there is not a greater purpose for your education. Therefore, I encourage you to place your educational goals in your plan, not your vision.

Again, the general guidelines to remember as you begin to define a Vision for yourself are to allow your vision to be:

* general enough to allow you flexibility in how to achieve the Vision.
* able to provide a long-range view (probably 15-20 years or more) of where you want to be in life.
* specific only to the degree that it does not limit your options for happiness and success.
* simple but well thought out.
* motivational and exciting to you!

DEFINING YOUR GOALS- A FEW ROLE MODELS

When you think about people like Tiger Woods, Oprah Winfrey, and Bruce Lee, you will find that they all have a common bond. Each of them had a vision of where they wanted to see themselves in the future. The vision they had was not just an ordinary vision of *"what I want to be when I grow up."* Their visions, although each very different, reflected inner strengths and allowed them to make the most of their unique talents in everything they did. Their visions served as motivators that gave them a foundation and a direction that they believed would give their lives special meaning.

Tiger Woods once told a reporter that his goal in life was to make the world see life differently through golf. This is powerful because his vision went beyond the limited scope of winning a particular golf tournament or being perceived as a leading golfer. His vision was much more motivating because he talked about the impact of his actions on the world at large.

Since I never had a chance to speak with Tiger Woods personally, I can't say for sure why he chose this statement as the motivator for his actions, but from all that I know about him and his sense of drive and determination, I feel confident that for Woods, having a vision like this helped give meaning to his life. In his case, winning a particular tournament or being a top golfer alone would not be enough incentive to drive all of those

47

hours of practice and sacrifice. I believe he had to find something that was personally motivating to him that would keep him focused during good and bad times. Therefore, Tiger's vision embodies a part of who he is and helps him establish himself on his own terms.

A good example to illustrate the difference between tangible accomplishments and ultimate outcomes is the way Oprah Winfrey defines her life goals. Most of us see Oprah as an extremely talented and successful television talk show host. She is considered to be one of the most successful and wealthy people in the world. However, Oprah does not define her life goal as being a leading television talk show host. Her goal in life is to bring about meaningful changes in people's lives throughout the world. Being a television host is her profession (part of her plan), but it is only a means of achieving her vision of bringing about "change in people's lives."

To further illustrate the point, there was a time that Oprah was going to quit her job as a TV host. However, when she realized the full impact that her show was having on people's lives she decided to stay. Therefore, if there ever came a time that she felt her show was not changing lives; I believe she would move on and do something else that she thought might be more meaningful. Currently we know that in addition to hosting her TV show, she is an entrepreneur, movie producer, actress, and founder of a school for girls in South Africa. She continues to live her vision through all of these endeavors. Oprah then is personally successful because of her impact, not because of her position.

It is also important to keep in mind that your vision can come in many different formats and inspiration can be found in some of the least likely places. In 1999, when I was in Singapore with my wife and son, we went to eat lunch at the Planet Hollywood on Orchard Road, a key shopping district in Singapore. In one of the main dining areas I noticed on the wall a framed, handwritten note. When I walked over to it, I saw that it was a reproduction of Bruce Lee's vision. He entitled it "My Definite Chief Aim," and it was handwritten in January 1969. Since I always felt that Bruce Lee was one of the greatest martial artists and I love his movies, I read it and later wrote it down on the back of my placemat. Let me share it with you.

(Secret)

My Definite Chief Aim

I, Bruce Lee, will be the first highest paid Oriental super star in the United States. In return I will give the most exciting performances and render the best of quality in the capacity of an actor. Starting 1970 I will achieve world fame and from then onward till the end of 1980 I will have in my possession $10,000,000. I will live the way I please and achieve inner harmony and happiness.

Bruce Lee

Jan. 1969

(Secret)

It appears that he wrote this statement in the form of a secret contract with himself. Sometimes thinking of something as a secret makes you more intent on protecting it. Although Bruce Lee did not live to the end of the 1980s, it seems that he wrote this vision in a way that motivated him. I don't know what his personal fortune ended up being, but I do know that his performances were so exciting that even today, more than thirty years after his death, many still see him as the authority in martial arts, and his movies are still some of the most popular martial arts films ever made. It is rare to find martial artists or anyone who has achieved the kind of fame that he has achieved. Another interesting point is that "My Definite Chief Aim" never mentioned anything about martial arts. Therefore, martial arts was simply a vehicle to achieving his ultimate goal. It was a part of the plan as opposed to his complete vision.

Now that you understand the importance of your vision and you have been presented with a range of ways that it can be created, it is up to you to develop your own unique vision in your own unique style. Take your time and really search your inner self in terms of what would give you happiness, purpose, and meaning in life. To measure the effectiveness of your vision statement, you should ask yourself the following questions:

- When I think of my vision, does it motivate me?
- Is it meaningful enough to motivate me during tough times?
- Is my vision a little scary and will it make me stretch my own abilities?
- Do I believe I can do it? Why?
- How often do I think this vision statement will change?

(Although it is fine to change and modify your vision, it should not be done too frequently.) If you have a good vision statement, it should be able to stand the test of time unless major life changes and new life revelations cause you to shift its focus.

Now that you have taken the first step in the Frazier Formula For Success we suggest that you take a little time to let the vision sink in. As we move into the next chapter, we will discuss how to develop "The Plan" and how important this next step is when turning your vision into your reality!

CHAPTER 3

Crafting a Plan

Refining Your Strategy

Now that you have defined the vision of what you want to achieve in life, it's time to develop the plan for how you're going to get there. While the vision paints a picture of your ultimate goal; it is the plan that draws out a map of the route you will take. A vision without a *plan* is like traveling to a place you have imagined or heard about without clear directions. Just as you need a roadmap to guide you when you're driving in an area you're not familiar with, having a life plan is crucial if you want to increase your chances for success.

Your plan can be as simple or complex as you need it to be. If your vision is pretty direct, then most likely your plan will also be fairly straightforward. Even if your plan seems to be based on standards and goals that seem fairly universal, consider the elements of your vision that drive you to reach beyond the scope of what other people normally do. It may be worthwhile spending extra time developing a plan that can give you a competitive advantage. Typically, an effective plan is one that will position you to reach your vision in the time period that you designate. It should be well thought out, flexible, and achievable. There should also be short-term and long-term components to your plan. Consider some advice offered by Jim Collins in his book, *Good To Great (2001)*. Although he is writing about companies for a business audience, the ideas are easily applicable to your personal process. His "Hedgehog Concept" encourages us to delve deeper into our process by asking questions about the things we are deeply passionate about. It's asking ourselves about what we as individuals can be the best in world at and what kinds of things drive our economic engine.

Developing your personal plan is not unlike developing an organizational plan. For example, the organization that I am most responsible for leading these days is called the Hill House Association. As we went through our strategic planning process a couple of years ago, we started by looking at our mission and vision statements. By conducting a formalized "needs assessment," we asked ourselves critical questions such as what needs are we currently meeting, what are the unmet needs, what types of services are we uniquely positioned to deliver value on, and what future trends do we anticipate. Through a process that engaged our various stakeholders, we then used this information to update our Mission, Vision and Values Statements. Based on our vision, we built a plan for Hill House that took into consideration our organizational strengths and weaknesses, as well as the types of opportunities and threats that exist within the context of our environment. Therefore, the plan that we built was directly aligned to help us achieve our Vision by taking advantage of our own uniqueness as a community-based agency.

In your personal planning process, keep in mind preparation and training appropriate to every aspect of your vision. For example, if your Vision includes a high level of professional achievement, then your plan should probably include some details about your formal education plans – which might include college and advanced training. If you plan a career in the entertainment field, you should plan on receiving proper training and finding increasingly challenging performance opportunities. If your vision includes community activities, then your plan should outline as specifically as possible the form those activities might take, such as volunteering in the food bank or coaching a basketball team at the youth center. For every type of plan and for nearly every goal, some type of training, and certainly some preparation, is necessary, so let's get to work...

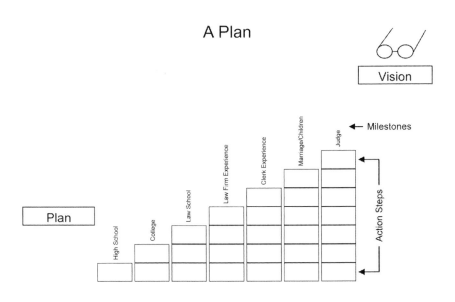

The Frazier Formula for Success ®

A Plan

A-3

What makes the Plan in the Frazier Formula For
Success™ different from other plans is that it can take into
account personal and professional goals. In developing this plan
you will take into consideration your strengths and weaknesses
as you chart your path to success. Outside opportunities and
threats will also be examined and incorporated into your overall
plan. At the end of this chapter, you should have all the tools
you need to create a life plan for yourself that will help you to
achieve your ultimate vision. No matter how simple or how
complex your vision might be, this chapter will help you to
better understand a personal planning process that can help you
to be successful.

As with any worthwhile plan, there is an evolutionary
process in which you are constantly updating and enhancing
your plan. The thought and thoroughness that you put into the
planning process will pay off once your initial plan is
completed. Keep in mind, the best plans tend to be simple,
creative, and well thought out. It is not important that everyone
you know understands the plan that you put together; it has to
make sense mainly to you. There may be parts of your plan that
you will want to share with people whom you trust and respect,
and other components of your plan that you will want to keep to
yourself. Remember that this is your vision, and your choices
can protect and develop your plan as you need. As we will
discuss later, keeping your ideas confidential during the

developmental stages requires you to be solely responsible for your plan. However, it does not hurt to listen to other creative ways that people use to achieve particular goals.

Most of the time, there is more than one way to achieve a stated goal; therefore, it is important to select a pathway that you are comfortable with and one that will allow you to have some of the life experiences that you desire along the way. The journey toward achieving your vision is often as important as your final destination. Therefore, how you achieve your vision is equally as important as what your vision happens to be. It is sometimes helpful to think of your plan as the steps you can take to position yourself to achieve your Vision. We will talk more about the whole concept of positioning as we start to learn about the Frazier Formula Planning Format.

Now that you have a general idea of where we are going with the planning process, let's get started on creating a plan for you. You might want to take notes and start to create your plan as we move along. This of course assumes that you already have a vision that you can use as a guideline.If you don't have a clear vision, simply read this chapter now and come back to it later after you have a vision statement and are ready to create your plan.

The first step in the planning process is to take a few minutes to list your *strengths* and *weaknesses*. In your notes, create two columns, and under the heading _Strengths_ list any personal characteristics, skills, special abilities, and talents that you possess. A strength can even be something seemingly simple that you do well, like greeting other people in the street or planning an organized grocery list. In contrast, under the heading _Weaknesses_ be sure to list any personal characteristic that you perceive to be a weakness – things you don't feel you do particularly well. You might want to remember feedback that you received from employers, parents, friends, or spouses to see if those comments reveal any strengths or weaknesses that might not be immediately obvious to you. Be open and honest and treat this exercise without judgment because you are simply listing these factors for your own benefit.

These lists that you are creating should be completely confidential since you don't necessarily want other people to know all of your strengths and weaknesses. This knowledge of yourself is vitally important not just for the planning process, but as you make commitments and decisions throughout your life.

It is also important to identify any key weaknesses that you might need to turn into strengths in order to reach your vision. It is always better to be aware of the areas where you need to improve so that you can do something about them. However, improving your weaknesses is no substitute for standing on your strengths. In today's competitive world, building on your strengths gives you a far greater advantage in your quest for success. Your weaknesses can be reduced through hard work, but it's not always worthwhile to expend energy that could be used promoting your strong points and focusing your efforts in directions where your strengths will pay dividends.

Below are sample lists of strengths and weaknesses that can be used as models.

STRENGTHS	WEAKNESSES
Social Skills	Difficult to work with
Communication Skills	Weak communication skills
Foreign Language Skills	Non-analytical
Speed reading	Slow Reader
Good memory	Lack Discipline
Analytic Ability	Easily Distracted
Public Speaking	Fear of Public Speaking
Mathematics	Not good at math
English Literature	Weak language skills
Understand finances	Poor financial planning
Patient	Impatient
Compassionate	Self-Absorbed
Resourceful	Procrastinator
Self-Control	Lazy
Athletic	Easily Overcommitted

Take a few minutes to refer back to your vision statement. When you think of your vision, what different opportunities exist for people to achieve that vision? List your answers under a heading entitled _Opportunities_. Be sure to take your time and be creative in thinking about all the possible paths that one can take to achieve the vision that you stated, and don't limit yourself to the path or various paths that you plan to take. The key is to brainstorm without committing to any of the opportunities that you are listing.

After you have listed the opportunities, make another heading entitled _Threats_. Under _Threats_, list anything that you can think of that might be a roadblock to achieving your Vision. Again, take your time and be thoughtful. This could include external factors that impact relationships, work, personal beliefs, skill requirements, etc. List potential Threats even if you are not sure that they apply to you specifically.

Below are some examples of Opportunities and Threats that one might list.

OPPORTUNITIES

There is a need for public servants
Public recently become aware of a particular need
Minority percentage in field needs to be greater
Few people think about this profession
Media field looks for people with charisma

Readiness for Change
Low Barriers to Entry
New Technology will be required
Growing public interest in subject or field

THREATS
Resistance to Change
Racism
Sexism
Classism
Low demand for profession
Over-supply of workers/competitors
Job may become Obsolete
Technology Changes
Too Many Commitments
Political bureaucracy
Lack of funding
Lack of support

Once you have listed your own Strengths, Weaknesses, Opportunities and Threats, the next step is to connect your Strengths with Opportunities and your Weaknesses with your Threats. Try linking them in such a way as to see if any of your strengths complement the different Pathways or Opportunities for achieving your Vision. This will be important when you actually select a particular direction you want to take to achieve your Vision. Below are a few examples of Strengths which complement Opportunities.

Strengths	**Opportunities**
Communication Skills	Public Speaking can be a powerful plus
Entrepreneurial	Industry is Open to New Ideas and Innovation

The results of the linkages should give you a sense of which Pathways might be most advantageous based upon your individual strengths. This is what is meant by selecting a plan that builds upon your strengths.

Next, link your weaknesses with the threats. To do this, think of which of your weaknesses directly relates to the threats that currently exist. This can reveal valuable information to you as you start your planning process. In particular, it will let you know which of your weaknesses are most important for you to work on so they do not hinder your progress toward achieving your vision. Below are some examples of linked weaknesses and threats.

Weaknesses	**Threats**
Impatient	Years of training required
Easily Offended/Thin-Skinned	Requires working with public
Non-creative	Many competitors in your field
Computer Illiterate	Changing technology is essential
Lack of Faithfulness in Relationships	Public always looking for scandal
Arriving on Time is a Challenge	Early mornings are required for success

One of the benefits of this exercise is that it helps you to become aware of the areas that could pose difficulties or roadblocks on your journey to success. This can be beneficial to you in that it allows you to know what some of your limitations and challenges are enabling you to balance them in other ways. For example, perhaps you are in business but you are not very good at accounting and finance. Since you know this is not an area of strength, you might want to select a partner who has this expertise. Further, having an understanding of the weakness/threat linkages can let you know when you should ask for assistance from someone else who is strong in this area. Once you recognize your strengths and weaknesses in the context of opportunities and threats, you are able to carry out other strategic elements of your plan.

The reality in life is that we all have strengths and weaknesses. Even those people who we consider to be extremely successful have weaknesses. Therefore, the key for all of us is to try to manage and strengthen our weaknesses so that they do not hinder us from reaching our dreams.

The process you've just completed is popularly known as a SWOT Analysis, which stands for strengths, weaknesses, opportunities, and threats. Some scholars and business professionals such as George A. Steiner in his book, _Strategic Planning_, would refer to it as WOTS Up analysis but ultimately, regardless of terminology, it is a method by which to evaluate the most essential steps in strategic planning. These principles can help you plan your direction, and can be helpful in completing the personal planning process.

The next stage in the planning process is to select your strategic direction based upon your strengths and opportunities. Try to determine one, two, or possibly three main _Pathways_ you want to follow to achieve your vision. I call these _Pathways_, because they clarify how you will accomplish your goals. Allow your vision to include _tangible_ active pathways to ensure that you can successfully achieve your vision. A Pathway addresses _how_ you will emphasize your strengths and interests. An example might be something like this:

Vision: To become a movie star and champion of worthy charities
Pathways: Acting
Singing
Civic Awareness/Involvement

Once you have determined your key Pathways, it is time to transfer your ideas into the Frazier Formula Planning Format. The format is as follows:

Vision Statement
Pathways
Long-Range Position Statement
Position Categories
Action Steps (Short-term and Long-term)

After discussing the Planning Format, The Frazier Formula Time Matrix will be explained. Allow yourself to go through each stage in the Planning Format without being overly concerned about timelines. Feel free to keep notes about future aspects of your planning while concentrating on each step in turn.

First, transfer the Vision that you created for yourself onto the top of a sheet of paper. Below it, identify your Pathways. Based upon your Vision and personal Pathways, you will want to create a long-term Position Statement. This position statement should encompass not only your professional goals but any personal achievements you are striving toward in life. For example, your combined personal and professional goal might be "to position myself to be a top public official while maintaining a healthy home life." Another example could be "to position myself internationally as a dancing sensation and to leverage this to participate in movies while maintaining a personal sense of balance." Think about the position statement as determining what overall position would be needed to best achieve the vision.

After satisfactorily crafting your Long-Range Position Statement, the Position Categories should be set up to assist you in reaching your desired position. Allow the position categories to be broad enough in their definition that they can cover all the main areas where you feel you need to take action steps to reach your ultimate vision. For example, typical position categories might be Education, Work, Community, or Personal. More unique or specialized position statements could include Drama, Religion, Family, Publications or many others depending on your own sense of priorities. One of the position categories that I personally use is called Innovate and Inspire. In this position category, I include the very book you are reading -- Most Likely to Succeed happens to be a significant action step in my personal plan. I suggest that three to five Position Categories will be adequate for most people. However, there is no limit since your entire plan depends on you and how you personally wish to shape your plan. To give you a better idea of how Position Categories can be used, below is an example.

Position Statement: Enter the entertainment business by leveraging talents in dance while maintaining a sense of balance in life.

Position Categories

Dancing   Acting   Academic   Personal

Once you have selected the position categories that you wish to use, it is now time to put your action steps under each one. The action steps can be short-term or long-term in nature. For now, don't worry about when each action needs to happen. Simply list all of the action steps you feel you should take under each of the categories to achieve your position statement and ultimately your vision. There is no limit to the number of action steps you can have under each position category. Your steps do not have to be "definite," they can be "if possible" or "under consideration." Consider becoming president of a nonprofit agency if the right opportunity presents itself or possibly attending an Ivy League University. The steps for each goal must be clear and in some way tangible. The amount of creativity that you put into your action steps will ultimately pay off by allowing you to identify unique opportunities that others might overlook.

Since you have now had a chance to review the Frazier Formula Planning Format, let's take a look at a completed format in its entirety.

Frazier Formula Planning Format (An Example)

Vision Statement: To become a movie star and be well known throughout the world.

Pathways: Dancing   Acting

Position Statement: Position self to enter the movie business by leveraging talents in dance and acting while continuously maintaining a sense of balance in life.

Position Categories: Dancing
Acting
Education
Personal

Let's take a few minutes to review Step Two of the Frazier Formula For Success™, The Plan. The following steps are necessary to complete the plan as outlined in this chapter.

- Make sure you are comfortable with your vision statement.
- Make a list of personal strengths and weaknesses.
- Make a list of opportunities and threats to achieving your vision.
- Link your strengths and opportunities to determine your core strategies.
- Link your weaknesses and threats to determine key areas to enhance.

Complete the Frazier Formula Planning Format
- Vision Statement
- Pathways
- Long-Range Position Statement
- Position Categories
- Action Steps (Short and long-term)

The next course of action is to complete The Frazier Formula Time Matrix. This process allows you to really think through each

stage in your plan according to the time it will take to complete it. Typically, the time frames most useful are as follows:
- Long-Term
- Mid-Term
- Short-Term
- Ongoing
- Already Completed

Review your action steps to ensure consistency with vision and position statement. Date your work and keep it in a private location.

In beginning to think through examples of how two very different people might engage the Frazier Planning Format and the accompanying Frazier Time Matrix, consider what conditions would need to be considered for each. The example is from a person who desires to be a great dancer and movie actor. For this person, there are a range of approaches that might be taken to the Planning Format most of which involve education, training and experience in the fields of dance and film. We use this example to highlight some of the nuances in developing the plan. The great thing about putting together personal and professional plans is that there are no right or wrong answers. It is simply a matter of how you as an individual choose to achieve your vision.

As you read each of the following samples, imagine how a person with that same vision could have a completely different plan. It is all about how you as an individual want to achieve your goal and how you clarify it so that you are building upon your individual strengths to achieve your life ambitions. After you read through the samples, you will be ready for the third and final component of the Frazier Formula For Success™ - The Right Attitude.

SAMPLE I
Frazier Formula Planning Format

Vision Statement: To become a movie star and be well known throughout the world.

Pathways: Dancing   Acting

Position Statement: Position self to enter the movie business by leveraging talents in dance and acting while continuously maintaining a sense of balance in life.

Position Categories with Action Steps:
Dancing:
- Create new dance steps

- Possibly develop a new style of dance
- Research history of dance in movies
- Become recognized for exciting dance performances
- Understand current dance trends
- Volunteer to arrange and choreograph productions and performances
- Teach dance classes
- Seek professional dance positions

Acting:

- Volunteer as extra in movies
- Attend networking socials and industry parties
- Participate in dance roles for plays, musicals, etc.
- Frequent areas where movies are often filmed
- Study why actors become selected for movies
- Enter national competitions such as Star Search
- Create own amateur movie which has dance focus
- Act in commercials and photo shoots
- Build acting portfolio
- Participate in school productions

Education:

- Attend schools known for performing arts
- Take acting courses
- Take formal dance classes

- Take marketing oriented classes to learn how to market myself better

Personal:

- Maintain an attractive appearance
- Pray and meditate to maintain balance
- Consider moving to certain regions of the country/world where dance and acting talent can be recognized
- Maintain contact with dance professionals
- Make sure my professional relationships don't become too personal
- Make sure my personal relationships don't compromise my profession ambition
- Contact successful alumni in my field
- Share my experience and enthusiasm for the arts with interested youth

By now you should have a good grasp of how to do your own life planning within the context of the Frazier Formula Planning Format. Once you have completed the format for yourself, there is an additional step that you can take to help you organize your action steps within appropriate time frames. This can be done through the Frazier Formula Time Matrix. To lay out the matrix, place position categories on one axis and the following time variables on the other:

Short-Term, Medium-Term, Long-Term, Ongoing, and Already Completed.

Once you have set up your worksheet, it is time for you to transfer all of your action steps from the Frazier Formula Planning Format into the Frazier Formula Time Matrix. Take time to really think about each element in turn to establish the duration of each time frame in relation to your goals. You will need to determine and indicate concrete time frames for each Action Step. For example Short-Term (< 2 years), Mid-Range (2-8 years), Long-Term (> 8 years). You can simply use these time frames or select your own based upon what makes the most sense for you. If you need more space within a particular category, simply expand your matrix to fit your needs.

Using the earlier example of the woman who wanted to become a judge, the following presents a version of her completed time matrix.

Once you have reviewed the diagram on the following page, establish your template for your matrix and apply position categories.

Now you are on your way to the next component of the Frazier Formula for Success, "Cultivating the Right Attitude."

Frazier Formula Time Matrix

Position Categories

	EDUCATION	WORK	PERSONAL
Long-Term (> 8 Years)	Educate self about judicial processes and pathways	Become highly regarded legal professional Seek appointment or run for judge seat	Maintain strong family relationships Consider marriage and having kids
Mid-Term (2-8 Years)	Acceptance and completion of Law School Study to pass Bar Exam	Seek entry attorney position at an established law firm or corporation Clerk for a judge in field of interest	Join a weekend band Become member of health club
Short-Term (< 2 Years)	Complete College with honors Prepare for LSAT exam	Participate in moot court exercises Seek Summer Internships	Learn to play guitar Volunteer at community center
Ongoing:	Reading general and legal news to keep informed	Develop relationships with lawyers/judges	Maintain integrity and health Take time with mentors
Already Completed:	Accepted to college Completed Freshman & Sophomore years in college	Determine legal areas of interest	Use Frazier Formula as a tool Drafted personal vision statement

CHAPTER 4

CULTIVATING THE RIGHT ATTITUDE

ALIGNING YOUR OUTLOOK

The Right Attitude is perhaps the most important component to the Frazier Formula For Success™ . Attitude is very often what makes the difference between success and failure. Having the right attitude keeps you focused on your vision and allows you to work your plan even when times are tough. And since we all are bound to have hard times in life, having the Right Attitude can make the difference for all of us. The Frazier Formula For Success™ is simply not complete without the Right Attitude.

Before we go farther, let's take a few moments to define "the Right Attitude." My definition of attitude is fairly broad. I see attitude as a combination of an individual's mood, perspective, orientation, and outlook towards goals, other people, and self. Therefore, "the Right Attitude" represents the ideal combination of these elements directed toward a particular vision, industry, job, goal, or even specific situation. This suggests that there is a right attitude for different people, places, and things. For example, an assertive attitude on the job might not translate well in a family situation. While it is true that the right attitude is different based on the circumstances, there are certain attitudes that we should all strive to possess in order to be successful.

Self-confidence and perseverance are examples of attributes that should be a part of the right attitude for everyone. Regardless of industry, occupation, or vision, self-confidence and perseverance are elements that can help anyone to be successful.

A positive perspective is another attribute that cuts across circumstances to be a part of "the Right Attitude" in almost all cases. There are other components of attitude that can be useful in all situations. Which ones can you think of? *(see diagram A-4)*

The Frazier Formula for Success ®

The Right Attitude

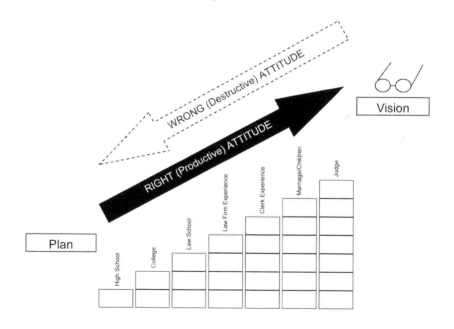

A-3

Have you ever heard of the Rocky Bleier story? Rocky Bleier was a running back for the Pittsburgh Steelers when they won four Super Bowls back in the 1970s. But his road to success was not an easy one.

Rocky was a talented college football star who worked really hard to prove himself as a star athlete. His dream was realized when he was drafted to the Pittsburgh Steelers in 1968. The same year however, he was drafted again; this time by the U.S. Army for the war in Vietnam. While in Vietnam he won a Purple Heart and numerous other awards for bravery including the Bronze Star. Tragically, in the process of assisting a fellow soldier, he was shot in the leg. The bullet somehow severed important nerves and he was told by his doctor that he would never walk again. Initially he was devastated by the news because he had planned to return to the United States to continue to play professional football. Rocky refused to accept that fate, and kept his Vision of playing pro football. He sought out expert advice and developed a Plan to strengthen his legs so he could walk, then later run. The amount of personal will that it took to keep him on his plan was incredible. Through his determination and the support of Art Rooney (then owner of the Steelers), he not only was able to walk and run, he was re-signed by the Steelers in 1970 and placed on the active roster in 1972. Securing his status on the "Dream Team", Rocky Bleier and Franco Harris, became the first pair of running backs to go over 1,000 yards rushing in a single season in 1976. He retired in 1980 and has since focused on using his experiences to motivate others worldwide. It's clear to me that Rocky Bleier had the right attitude to keep moving toward his vision. Without that attitude, his final outcome would surely have been different.

I have found through life experiences that when everything else is equal, it is attitude that makes the difference. Whether it's competition on the court or in the office, attitude tends to be the great equalizer. When I was a teenager, I can remember my karate sensei, or teacher, telling the class about Bill "Superfoot" Wallace, one of the most successful kick boxers of all time. My sensei attended one of Bill Wallace's seminars where he learned some of his techniques and philosophy. One of the things that Wallace shared was that very often when he was fighting his opponents, they were equally as strong and as fast as he was. The difference between Bill Wallace and his opponents was mainly in attitude. When his opponents threw a kick, they thought to themselves "let me throw this kick and hope it will connect." Superfoot trained himself to expect that the technique would work and never let doubt become a part of his thought pattern. "Superfoot" Wallace indeed had the right attitude to be successful in his competitions.

Another example of how attitude makes the difference can be seen in the process of breaking wooden boards. Although this was a very rare practice in our dojo (karate school), on one such occasion I recall learning how to break a board. I was very surprised to learn that it was more mental than physical. It was all about where you placed your focus and your personal attitude. The key was to place your focus beyond the board and to have confidence that your hand or foot will move beyond the wood, breaking the board in the process. Very often people would yell in a certain way called kiai ("show of spirit") to help them to generate energy and momentum. Through this experience, I learned that having the right attitude to break boards included having confidence and a willingness to focus beyond the target.

One of the most important elements of the Right Attitude is persistence. This means never giving up. It means learning from our mistakes and sticking with something until it's done right. A favorite book of mine, *The Greatest Salesman in the World* by Og Mandino, puts it very nicely:

"I will persist until I succeed. I was not delivered unto this world in defeat, nor does failure course in my veins. I am not a sheep waiting to be prodded by my shepherd. I am a lion and I refuse to talk, to walk, to sleep with the sheep....The slaughterhouse of failure is not my destiny. I will persist until I succeed."

As you think about executing your career plan to move toward achieving your vision, be sure to keep in mind that it will be extremely difficult without the right attitude. If you remember the movie "Jerry Maguire," you may recall a valuable lesson in how the football player named Rod Tidwell (played by Cuba Gooding, Jr.) had the vision and even a working plan; however, his attitude was not quite right. His vision was to obtain "quan" which was the term he created for the complete superstar package of fame and fortune. Tidwell was an intense player on the field, but he was too focused on the money ("Show me the money!") and did not allow himself to enjoy the game. Although his statistics were excellent, he was still not getting the attention that he desired. Finally, Jerry Maguire told him that his bad attitude was holding him back from new heights of success. Once Tidwell absorbed this and his personal outlook changed, he was able to find the "quan" he was looking for. Therefore, having the right attitude made all the difference for him to achieve his vision.

Just as he learned the right attitude from Maguire, Rod Tidwell was able to teach Maguire a very valuable lesson about the importance of relationships. His guidance allowed Maguire to commit fully to his relationship with his girlfriend, and to utter the second most memorable line from the movie – "You complete me."

This same concept of the right attitude can be applied to relationships. In many ways, successful relationships require the right attitude more than anything else. Relationships are very delicate. Whether they are friendships or love relationships, they all require special care. What can take weeks, months, or years to build up can be destroyed in a few moments of the wrong attitude. Often I find that mistakes are made not because you don't know what the right attitude needs to be, but that you might be busy or focused on something else and don't take the time and energy to apply it. Therefore, you might send the wrong message because of your attitude. In other circumstances, particularly when it relates to romance, people become confused as to what the right attitude for this relationship and situation should be.

With all this talk about the right attitude and how it can be different depending on the situation, you're probably wondering "How do I know what the right attitude is for my situation?"

The first step is to adopt the "universal" right attitudes that you feel can apply to almost any situation. For starters, that means having a positive outlook, an attitude of perseverance and confidence in yourself. Once you have determined what your universal attitudes will be, try to find ways to improve any of them that are not naturally your strengths. Remember, the universal attitudes are going to be used time and time again and should be a permanent part of who you are. Take the time to consciously develop each specific component. If you have a difficult time being positive, then find a way to practice identifying the good side of any situation you face. Perhaps perseverance is not your strong point. If so, train yourself in small ways not to quit until the job is complete or until you are successful. As you continue this practice, these attributes will start to become habits. Once you have cultivated them into habits, they instinctively become part of your permanent attitude.

Second, after you adopt the universal right attitudes, learn to assess each specific situation. If you are going in for a job interview, you know that certain attitudes can be helpful in almost all interviews. An attitude that punctuality, hard work, and proven results are important won't steer you wrong during most interviews. In addition, if you take the proper time to understand the organizational or industry culture, you can determine other components of attitude that might be helpful in a given company or institution. Companies within the hospitality industry such as hotels, restaurants, and other service organizations typically are looking for people who embrace the concept that being "people oriented" and "hands on" are part of the right attitude.

If you are in a situation such as an interview where you have time to prepare yourself and your attitude, you might want to think of personal examples of how each component of the right attitude has applied to your life. Other situations may not afford you with this luxury.

The application of the right attitude goes way beyond job interviews. It can be applied to your vision, education, personal relationships, family, sports, and many other situations. Once again, to determine the right attitude for the situation, first adopt the universal right attitude. Next, assess each specific situation to determine the expected right attitudes, and finally, decide on which components of attitude you will embrace for the specific situation.

One of the most important ways that mastering The Right Attitude can be helpful is when dealing with family. After all, success without family or close relatives to share it with is ultimately empty. Even when a family member is trying to help you, or you are trying to help them, it is often met with resistance and ingratitude. Families face many challenges, but they are so important that I think it's worthwhile to determine how some of the universal Right Attitudes can be applied.

I believe that a forgiving spirit should be a part of the Right Attitude when dealing with family. Holding grudges produces a spirit of negativity, and this spirit of negativity can spread to all those around you. It can even manifest itself in the lives of your children. The way that you handle situations will guide your children. Whether you like it or not, your children will pick up your habits, both bad and good. Also, whether you realize it or not, holding grudges and letting this negative energy fester within you holds you back from more freely enjoying life.

You may know the song by Will Smith called "Just the Two of Us." It has also been made into a book for children. In the context of providing wise counsel to his son, he talks about not letting bad people or bad experiences get you down.

"Throughout life people will make you mad
Disrespect you and treat you bad.
Let God deal with the things they do
'Cause hate in your heart will consume you too."

Another key component to the right attitude when dealing with family is maintaining a perspective of continuous love and support. It is possible to be angry with someone but still have love and support for them. One of the greatest benefits of family is a sense of unconditional belonging and always knowing that help is nearby regardless of the situation. Therefore, I believe that the Right Attitude for dealing with family is a forgiving spirit as well as continuous love and support. Even if this overall attitude is not reciprocated by all members of your family, at least it will allow you to be free. What other components of attitude would you add to this equation?

Let me end this chapter on "The Right Attitude" by sharing with you an e-mail I received from my sister Janine when I was overseas in Asia. Although I was never able to find out who the original writer of the story was, I believe that it demonstrates a great lesson on the power of attitude.

"Read this, and let it really sink in... Then choose how you start your day tomorrow... Jerry is the kind of guy you love to hate. He is always in a good mood and always has something positive to say. When someone

would ask him how he was doing, he would reply 'If I were any better, I would be twins!' He was a unique manager because he had several waiters who had followed him around from restaurant to restaurant. The reason the waiters followed Jerry was because of his attitude. He was a natural motivator. If an employee was having a bad day. Jerry was there telling the employee how to look on the positive side of the situation.

"Seeing this style really made me curious, so one day I went up to Jerry and asked him, 'I don't get it! You can't be a positive person all of the time. How do you do it?'

"Jerry replied, 'Each morning I wake up and say to myself, Jerry, you have two choices today. You can choose to be in a good mood or you can choose to be in a bad mood. I choose to be in a good mood. Each time something bad happens, I can choose to be a victim or I can choose to learn from it. I choose to learn from it. Every time someone comes to me complaining, I can choose to accept their complaining or I can point out the positive side of life. I choose the positive side of life.'

"'Yeah, right, it's not that easy,' I protested.

"'Yes it is,' Jerry said. 'Life is all about choices. When you cut away all the junk, every situation is a choice. You choose how you react to situations. You choose how people will affect your mood. You choose to be in a good mood or bad mood. The bottom line: It's your choice how you live life.'"

The story goes on to explain that one day Jerry accidentally left the back door of the restaurant open. Armed robbers came in and during the process Jerry was shot. As he was being taken to the hospital, based on the looks that the doctors and nurses had on their faces, it did not look good. Here's the rest of the story as Jerry explained to his friend what happened in the hospital.

"'Well, there was a big burly nurse shouting questions at me,' said Jerry. 'She was asking if I was allergic to anything. 'Yes' I replied. The doctors and nurses stopped working as they waited for my reply. I took a deep breath then replied 'Bullets!' Over their laughter, I told them, "I am choosing to live. Operate on me as if I am alive, not dead."'

"Jerry lived thanks to the skill of his doctors, but also because of his amazing attitude. I learned from him that every day we have the choice to live fully. Attitude after all, is everything."

At the end of the e-mail I was presented with a choice. The message presented these options:

1. Delete this.
2. Forward it to people you care about.
Hope you will choose #2. I did.

Always remember, when it comes right down to it, your attitude is your choice! In the words of legendary football icon and entrepreneur, Franco Harris:

How you look at a situation is very important, for how you think about a problem may defeat you before you ever do anything about it. When you get discouraged or depressed, try changing your attitude from negative to positive and see how life can change for you. Remember, your attitude towards a situation can help you to change it—you create the very atmosphere for defeat or victory.

If you combine this powerful concept of the Right Attitude with your vision and plan, success is just a matter of time. You've already succeeded in looking at your life as a journey toward personal and professional fulfillment. Regardless of how you interpret success for yourself, having the Right Attitude is essential to taking the journey.

UNIT II

TAKING A CLOSER LOOK

Chapter 5

Support Anchors

Making the Formula Work For You

"Nothing will ever be attempted
if all possible objections must first be overcome."
~*Samuel Johnson*

Now that you've read *Unit I– Introducing the Frazier Formula for Success*, you have a general understanding of the power and components behind The Frazier Formula for Success. *Unit II – Taking a Closer Look* is designed to give you greater depth and understanding of the components to the Frazier Formula that can be easily overlooked but are essential in helping you to maximize the Frazier Formula as a tool for your personal and professional achievement.

The Frazier Formula success framework gives you a solid base on which to start your life and career planning that will make you "most likely to succeed." As a way to maximize your success and understanding of the Frazier Formula, there are some subtle points that are important to highlight that might be missed otherwise.

In Diagram B1, the components outlined in Unit II relate to the Frazier Formula by being foundational building blocks that help to support the success framework that you learned about in Unit I. Similar to Maslow's Needs Hierarchy, Unit II has components that will help to ensure your success in conjunction with the Frazier Formula Framework that you learned about in Unit I.

The Frazier Formula for Success ®

Frazier Formula Model with Support Anchors

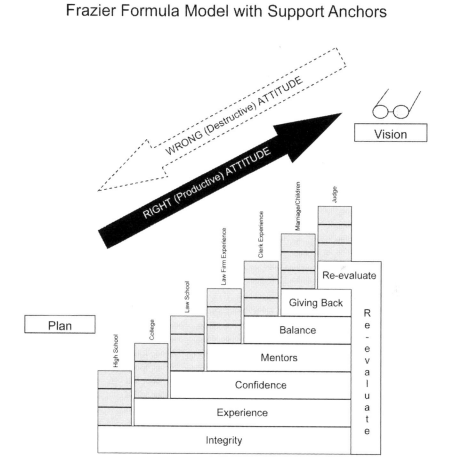

B-1

Each Chapter within Unit II will serve as a complement to the Frazier Formula in one or more ways. These insights will give you deeper insight on how to make the Frazier Formula for Success best work for you in your own circumstances. They will add a level of depth and understanding that is necessary to reinforce the key foundations supporting your efforts, and hopefully make you most likely to succeed.

Chapter 6

Maintaining Your Integrity

The importance of following strong principles

"Try not to be a man of success,
but rather be a man of value."
~Albert Einstein

Integrity is a vital part of success. In fact, there's really
nothing more important than maintaining your integrity. Part of
ensuring that you have The Right Attitude means that you are
focused on preserving the integrity of your vision and
maintaining integrity in everything that you do. It is one of the
essential building blocks of making the Frazier Formula work
for you. Therefore, it's up to you to protect it, preserve it, and
defend it.

Integrity is typically defined as sound moral principle,
uprightness, honesty, and sincerity. Another use of the word
integrity includes the state or quality of being complete;
unbroken, wholeness, or entirety. *(Webster)* When something
or someone has integrity we think of them as being complete –
having it all together and being trustworthy because they are
what they say they are. Both definitions apply to how I view
the importance of maintaining your integrity.

First, at the very foundation of success, integrity or being
honest, sincere, and of sound moral principle is a prerequisite to
building relationships, establishing trust or, more importantly,
being trustworthy. While we cannot always make others trust
us, we can always make sure that we are trustworthy as
individuals in our everyday actions and intentions. Anything

that requires building for the future becomes anchored when you become a person of integrity. It's becoming a man or woman of your word.

You can even argue that people cannot obtain "true" success if it means they have to compromise their integrity to achieve it. If we look to baseball, an example of this might be Barry Bonds who is the top homerun hitter in baseball history. He is recognized as a great athlete, however, due to his alleged steroid use which violates the ethics of baseball, it is likely that he will not get inducted into baseball's Hall of Fame. In fact, he could ultimately end up serving some time in prison for this type of unethical violation. Therefore, with all of his statistical success in baseball, material prosperity and fanfare, the questioning of his integrity will always cloud his extraordinary achievement. Take a moment to think about people you know of or have heard about who, once having their integrity questioned, have a very hard road overcoming it.

While the examples given are about famous athletes, these same principles of integrity apply to any of us on a day-to-day basis. If you are at your job and you do not develop a reputation for being honest and being a person of integrity, regardless of how talented you might happen to be, you will not be trusted with the keys to the office or greater responsibility for organizational oversight. Why would anyone promote you to partner if it is felt that you do not have a high degree of integrity? To do so would put the entire reputation of the firm or organization in jeopardy.

Does this mean that we have to be perfect? No. However, it means that we have to be constantly mindful of making sure that we have integrity each and every day. And if we fall off track, whether self-imposed or externally driven, we need to find ways to own up to it, correct the situation, and protect our integrity to the fullest extent possible.

Later in Unit II, you will read a chapter entitled "Multiple Mentors." What you will find out is that integrity is essential in forming meaningful mentoring relationships. The integrity needed applies to the mentee as well as the mentor. If the person being mentored is not trustworthy, it will be difficult for them to find mentors willing to be open to assisting them. Mentors are not going to be open and candid or even feel safe to share too much information if they do not have some trust or confidence in the person they are mentoring. If the mentor is not trustworthy, not only do they run the risk of leading others down the wrong pathway, mentees will pick up on this and will see the mentor's outreach as insincere. The bottom line is that healthy mentoring relationships require trust and integrity as foundational requirements.

Another way to view integrity deals with maintaining the wholeness or entirety of an organization, idea, or vision. One of the organizations closest to my heart is The National Society of Minorities in Hospitality (NSMH). NSMH was founded at Cornell University and is a national student-run organization designed to promote minority participation and advancement in the field of hospitality management. As its co-founder, I had the opportunity to serve in numerous leadership roles as a student including the role of National Chair. After college and becoming an alumnus of NSMH, for many years at our national conference elections, I would always ask the candidates running for national chair, "How will you maintain the *integrity* of NSMH?" My purpose in asking this question was to make sure that those running for the top position on the board understood the mission of NSMH and to make sure they understood it was their responsibility to preserve the "wholeness" or integrity of the organization's purpose.

I think it is important for each of us to ask the very same question of ourselves. How do you maintain the integrity or "wholeness" of your personal vision? It is extremely important that we are true to ourselves, our dreams, and aspirations. In addition, we want to make sure that our plans and the attitudes that we hold are consistent with integrity or wholeness and that there is trustworthiness in the way we pursue our dreams.

As you apply the Frazier Formula for Success to your life, be sure to take special time to understand the principles behind this chapter. Maintaining your integrity as it relates to your vision, plan, attitude and behavior as a whole is an essential building block to achieving your success.

Chapter 7

Learning From Your Experience

The value of persistence and resilience

*"Many of life's failures are people who did not realize how
close they were to success when they gave up."*
– Thomas Edison

One of the fundamental truths is that to be successful in
anything you have to be willing to work hard and overcome
obstacles. Nothing worthwhile comes easy in life. Clearly,
along the road there are bumps and bruises but life's winners are
those who push through, maintain their course, and do not allow
themselves to give up. And if you are a person who has high
ambition, achieving your goals will require more.

I remember driving to work one day and listening to the
Steve Harvey Radio Show in the morning. Steve Harvey is a
very talented comedian who has hosted several television shows
including It's *Showtime at the Apollo* and *The Steve Harvey
Show* which ran on the WB network from 1996 to 2002. Steve
stated that if you want to be successful in life and you want to
be "extraordinary," you have to do "extra." Then he gave a
number of examples of what qualifies as "extra," finally saying
that "extraordinary" without the "extra" leaves you with just
plain "ordinary." Not only was it comical because of the way
he tends to present his thoughts, it was particularly profound
although seemingly simple.

The Frazier Formula for Success is a tool designed to help you navigate through life, to find success, regardless of the obstacles you face. Sometimes finding success will require a different approach. At times it may mean reconsidering your goals or steps, but it always requires hard work and perseverance to take the extra steps that will move you from the ordinary to the extraordinary.

In your quest for success, overcoming obstacles can take many forms. What can you do if you are faced with discrimination? Perhaps because of your race or gender you have run into seemingly insurmountable roadblocks. As an African American, I recognize the inequities that Black people and other minority groups in our country face. There are barriers that discriminate against minority communities and often people who consciously and unconsciously hold stereotypes that make it extremely challenging to receive fair treatment. I could talk about the studies that have been conducted that show great disparities between the majority community and African Americans, Latinos, other minority groups and women in education, the workplace, our political and judicial system, and in our communities. I believe that it is essential to keep paying attention to and fighting for an equal playing field in the United States, and throughout the world. Nonetheless, I want to make it clear that none of these societal factors can hold you as an individual back from success unless you allow these things to become your crutch.

No matter what the circumstance might be, each of us as an individual has to be accountable for our own success. Granted, reaching your goal or fulfilling your vision may require an extra effort, more focus and creativity, greater flexibility, and a whole lot of energy. Nobody said that life was going to be fair or easy.

People are born in this world with all kinds of odds stacked against them. I think about Linda, a friend and mentor of mine. She was born with a rare neuromuscular disorder that causes progressive deterioration of voluntary muscles. From birth she was unable to walk; her muscles were not fully formed, and now, as an adult she is about a third of the size of you and me. Linda has an amazing background, a heart of gold, and she is extremely successful because she pushed herself to achieve in spite of her physical condition. When I first met Linda, she was the publisher of Executive Report Magazine, a civic leader, and chair of many prominent organizations. She later started her own consulting practice, and then became the CEO for the National Aviary in Pittsburgh. Whenever I think that I am overcommitted, I reflect on the fact that Linda has at least double the outside commitments that I have and she never seems to grow weary. While some may say that she was fortunate because she grew up with parents who had significant wealth, how many of us would have taken advantage of those opportunities and dedicated their life to having such a huge impact on this world, for both people and animals?

Another such example is Penny. Penny lives in the Hill District, a historic African American community in Pittsburgh. Like Linda, Penny needs to use a wheel chair to move around; however, Penny does not have the kind of financial resources Linda has – in fact, most would see her as poor. Several years ago after a physical attack, Penny was diagnosed with Amyotrophic Lateral Sclerosis (ALS), otherwise known as Lou Gehrig Disease. With diabetes and other medical challenges, Penny somehow manages to navigate throughout the neighborhood, because she is committed to making a difference in her community. Penny is active in her church and started a disability advocacy outreach ministry there. She prides herself on reaching out to others and being a fierce advocate to ensure that accessibility standards for people with disabilities in the Hill District are being met and improved. With very little money, she carries herself with pride and dignity because she knows that she is making a difference for herself and others.

A further example of perseverance can be seen in the case of Andrew Carnegie, who was one of the richest and most successful business people in American history. He made billions of dollars on the steel industry, but he gave new meaning to the phrase, "If at first you don't succeed, try, try again." Surprisingly, he was involved in more than 20 failing businesses before he hit on the company that became U.S. Steel Corporation.

The lesson he took from this, and so should we, is that making use of failures can be as simple as learning how not to do something the next time. We can learn from everything we do in life, including making mistakes. Most of the time we can make good decisions after thinking things over and talking to people we trust. Sometimes, even when we do things with the best of intentions they don't work out. The important thing is to learn from our experiences. We have to take lessons from our mistakes and rebound from adversity.

If we never made a move because we were afraid of failing, then we'd never make any progress. If we'd stopped trying after something went wrong, then we would never have learned how to ride a bicycle and man never would have walked on the moon. Remember what Og Mandino said about sticking with it: "I will persist until I succeed."

As we learn new things, we also have to be willing to look like beginners sometimes. Don't be afraid to look a little silly when you start something new. If you're trying hard and maintaining a positive attitude, then people will understand and be more willing to help you learn.

Ultimately, I don't believe that the opposite of success necessarily equals failure. Failure is a negative attitude. As long as you look at every experience as an opportunity to learn and move ahead, then you're still on the road to success.

CHAPTER 8

CONFIDENCE, NOT ARROGANCE

EARNING RESPECT FROM OTHERS,
NOT DEMANDING IT

"Greatness lies not in being strong,
but in the right use of strength."

- Henry Ward Beecher

A big part of maintaining the right attitude has to do with having the self-confidence to believe that you can achieve your vision. It's an essential ingredient for success. However, there's a fine line between confidence and arrogance. Confidence speaks to a firm belief in your own abilities. It's being certain or feeling a sense of assurance within. (Webster) On the other hand, arrogance is a sense of overbearing pride or self-importance. The dictionary also tells us that arrogance is being full of oneself due to unwarranted pride or self-importance.

Confidence is a state of mind that helps us overcome obstacles and make progress on our road to success. It's the internal belief that we can accomplish our goals. Our confidence shows itself to others as a positive outlook and a can-do approach to life. If we're confident, then we can make other people confident in our abilities. Confident people make good team players. Confident people make good leaders. Confident people are likely to be successful. Confidence builds character while arrogance takes away from character.

Sometimes confidence will be mistaken for arrogance, but the two attitudes are quite different. Confident people believe in themselves, and they believe that they can succeed. Arrogant people believe that they are better than other people, and while they may experience some degree of success in life, they limit their support because many people are put off by arrogant attitudes.

I found that some people act in an arrogant fashion to cover up their weaknesses. Or perhaps they may be overly aggressive or talk down to people because they are insecure about themselves. And of course there are those individuals who, for whatever reason, feel that they are superior human beings and that the world revolves around them.

Either way, when you think about the right attitude for you, consider your vision and whether your vision requires you to be confident or arrogant. My guess is that attitudes of confidence will take you farther than an arrogant attitude, no matter what your vision might be. Therefore, if you find that you are the type of person who is not yet confident in your own abilities, instead of putting on an air of arrogance, admit to yourself your own insecurities and start working on ways to make yourself more confident. It's amazing that through hard work and determination, you can build your skills and confidence in almost anything you put your mind toward.

I have often heard people say that in competitive disciplines such as sports, you have to be cocky and arrogant if you want to be successful. They will mention athletes such as boxers or football players citing a need for arrogance in order to compete. This is where I think the confusion comes into play. I think it is important to ask ourselves whether their arrogance is the reason that they are successful or whether they are successful in their field in spite of having an arrogant attitude. You also have to consider that the showmanship and public relations value some entertainers get does not always reflect their true personality and what is inside of them.

Other people may have such confidence in themselves that they appear arrogant, but their underlying character is good. One example of this might be Muhammad Ali, the great boxer. In his article, "Muhammad Ali: The Quintessential American," John Walker expresses the popular perception of Ali and his attitude. He explains:

> *"In many ways Muhammad Ali is the 'Quintessential American.' In his stand for religious and racial freedom, for his humility, generosity, braggadocio, deep and abiding physical and mental courage, though always larger than life – Ali exhibited many typical and deep-rooted American traits. He struck a number of positively resonant notes in the American psyche, that make him now a revered person. His life also reflects and contributed to the changing attitude of Americans to Black athletes from the sixties to the present day."*

For many people, Ali was known for his arrogant attitude, which was often displayed when he was preparing for a big fight. He used it to psych out his opponents and to gain attention for his cause. But he also turned out to be a man of strong principle and good character. His efforts as an anti-war activist and human rights crusader continued long after his boxing career ended. So it's the internal attitude that makes the difference, and people will be able to tell the difference between true confidence and true arrogance.

Chapter 9

Multiple Mentors

Cultivating relationships for success

"They may forget what you said
but they will never forget how you made them feel."
— *Carol Butcher*

Mentoring is an essential component of success regardless of how lofty our dreams and aspirations might be. Mentoring is a term that we are all familiar with; however, we do not all view mentoring in the same way. Conventional wisdom will tell you that it is important to have a mentor in your life to give you good advice and support. I believe that this is partially correct. I have found that it is typically unrealistic to assume that one person can be or should have to be a mentor in every aspect of your life. I believe in "multiple mentorship," the idea of developing a team of mentors who can give you different perspectives and different types of expertise or support.

If you think about the many dimensions in your life from professional career planning, personal relationships, spiritual guidance, and assistance in specialized areas such as sports, art, or music, leaning on any one person for all of these things could be a bit much. When I think of professional mentoring, I believe that it is important to develop mentors both within your organization and externally. Your internal mentor(s) can give you good solid advice and support on how to navigate within your company or organization because they know the specific players and the culture that you are operating within. If you are fortunate to have a professional mentor at a senior level within your organization, there are often doors they can open for you that you did not even know were there. At the same time, it may be difficult for some internal mentors to tell you in a timely way when it is in your best interest to start looking for your next opportunity outside of the company. It is often your external mentors who will be able to give you a more arm's length viewpoint about your current job scenario and are more free to connect you to new career opportunities and to help you think about different options that you should consider.

As we discussed in *Chapter 3 – Crafting a Plan* and you will soon read about in *Chapter 10 – Finding the Balance*, it is important to pay attention to the personal aspects of your life as well. Therefore, we should also consider mentors who can help us stay healthy and solid on personal matters such as family, relationships, spiritual guidance, fitness, finances and perhaps even food. As I sought to complete this book, as a first time author I reached out to people who could provide mentoring support and guidance on writing and publishing.

Developing multiple mentors requires that you have a strategy for deliberately networking and putting yourself in a position where you are reaching out to others and so that others can reach out to you. Your networking strategy starts by looking at your immediate support system of family and friends. At times it means identifying someone who you admire and respect, approaching them, introducing yourself and asking them for guidance in a particular aspect of your life. Perhaps a teacher, coach, administrator, corporate executive, or pastor may come to mind as you start to think about mentors. Even an immediate boss can be a mentor; however, it is important that you recognize the limitations and potential conflicts that can exist. At other times it takes a friend or mentor to introduce you to another person who you might not have been able to reach on your own to play a mentoring role for you. And from time to time, you may be in a place where a formalized mentoring program exists where you can take advantage of this structure.

I have been very fortunate in being able to use all of the above approaches to develop a strong network of mentors throughout my life, starting with my parents, who when I was growing up seemed to know just about everyone around me. My father was a mobility instructor for the blind and my mother held a variety of positions throughout her career from teaching to real estate and financial services. In her retirement she became an elected public official. My family includes aunts and uncles around the world: from consultants and news anchors to musicians and ambassadors. My wife has developed a strong base through the private school network and through her side of the family there are lawyers, educators, and public servants. People who I have met through schools I attended, professional associations, church, athletics, and boards that I have served on have all contributed to developing my network of mentors. I also have a mentor in the martial arts, Marvin or "Sensei" as I often call him, who kept me encouraged and found creative ways to keep the martial arts alive within me, even when my schedule, between work and family, did not allow me to attend structured classes. The important thing is to start by using the resources around you to find mentors and generate opportunities.

As you think about using The Frazier Formula for Success to develop your own roadmap for achievement, it is important to build into your plan action steps that will allow you to be deliberate about developing your network of mentors. Mentors don't have to be in your local neighborhood or even in your city. With modern technology, you can maintain a relationship with mentors across the country or even halfway around the world.

It is also essential that our attitude towards mentors and being mentored is healthy and productive. We should always respect and have the highest degree of integrity when dealing with mentors, as referenced in *Chapter 5 – Maintaining Your Integrity.* It is important that we are open to the candid feedback, guidance, and direction that mentors provide. However, it is always up to us to step back and make decisions for ourselves and to take responsibility for the decisions that we make. Good mentors will always respect this and will not try to force us to do exactly as they say or advise us to do. And keep in mind, when you have multiple mentors, you may generate several different perspectives and receive conflicting advice on the same issue. I have found from experience that valued mentors come in all colors, shapes, sizes, and genders. As an African American I have found that it is difficult for white mentors to understand the complex cultural challenges that black people face, the same as it would be difficult for a male mentor to understand all of the unique gender challenges that women face. Therefore, it is important to use their wise counsel to expand our thinking, consider broader alternatives, and to use the assistance of mentors to open doors whenever possible. And as one of my mentors, Delorese, once advised me: various mentors do not need to know each other or even necessarily know about the existence of each other. Keep in mind, it is okay to have different mentors at various stages in your life.

In addition to embracing this concept of multiple mentors, it is my hope that you will take it upon yourself to consider being a mentor for others throughout your life. One of my mentors, Greg, would always tell me that the only thing that I owe him as a mentor is that I will turn around and do the same thing for others coming behind me. As you will read about in *Chapter 10 – Making Your Contribution*, giving back ultimately increases our success, and I believe that serving as a mentor is a great way to give back. For some of us who have been incredibly blessed with great mentors, being a mentor for others is in fact an obligation.

Chapter 10

Finding The Balance

Meshing the personal and professional

"I think a hero is an ordinary individual
who finds strength to persevere
and endure in spite of overwhelming obstacles.
- Christopher Reeve

Striking a balance in our lives is always important. Balance is what often solidifies feelings of success and it is intrinsic to any implementation of a plan. Imagine how you'd feel if you advanced to the pinnacle of your chosen profession and received all the accolades and financial rewards that you had ever dreamed of, only to find that your family life was in a shambles and your children were in trouble and angry at you for ignoring them. It doesn't matter how successful you are in one area if you have no balance to your life or to your plan. Without paying attention to balance the success you seek will not be completely fulfilled.

Never forget the importance of balancing your personal life with your professional life. Work hard at your job, but work equally hard at giving your family and friends the attention they deserve. Sometimes we take things for granted and forget that our personal life requires an equal amount of work. Personally, I know that even when I had a strong professional vision, there was a time in my life when I realized I needed to re-evaluate my vision to ensure that my professional aspirations were matched with my desire to develop and maintain a strong family. My own vision had to be revised to incorporate family directly in

the vision so that my plan could be in alignment. Balancing
each aspect of your life will ultimately make you a better person
and potentially add to your sense of success.

Even in ancient times, wise men talked about the
important connection between good emotional health and
physical health. Make sure to nurture your mind, body and spirit
as you move forward. In South Africa during the 1980s the
slogan, "the personal is political" became synonymous with the
women's movement, indicating the recognition of the need for
conscious balance between our personal lives and our
convictions. Similarly, ancient Chinese philosophy centers
around the idea of the connection between mind, body, and
spirit. The Greeks maintained the idea of the scholar/athlete
suggesting that the body and the mind need equal focus and
balance. Even the Sanskrit word "yoga" refers to the ultimate
state of being which is to literally "yoke" the mind, body and
spirit. With all of these international examples, we know that
the personal simply must complement the professional in order
to bring about long-lasting balance and ultimately, success.

I really appreciate the ideas expressed in *The Power of
Full Engagement* by Jim Loehr and Tony Schwartz. In their
chapter on "The Pulse of High Performances: Balancing Stress
and Recovery," they suggest the following guidance:

"Balancing stress and recovery is critical to high
performance both individually and organizationally." If we take

the time to think critically about how we use our energy and stay focused on distributing it equally among those most essential parts of our lives: physical, emotional, mental, and spiritual, it becomes much easier to maintain the right attitude. How you use your energy either strengthens your cultivation of right attitude or it hinders it. Attitude is like managing energy in your life – positive energy brings positive outcomes where negative energy can attract negative results.

CHAPTER 11

MAKING YOUR CONTRIBUTION

GIVING BACK TO THE COMMUNITY

*"Footprints on the sands of time are
not made by sitting down."*

- Anonymous

As you move ahead in life and more good things come to you, it's always important to give something back. You can donate money or goods, but sometimes the most valuable donation you can make is a gift of your time. You'll find that this attitude of generosity will repay you in more ways than you thought possible. Volunteers often say that they feel better than the people they're helping.

In this increasingly selfish world, it's important to remember that there are always people less fortunate than ourselves who could use our help. Making a difference in other people's lives builds character, it improves your confidence and your self-esteem, and it will improve your chances of success. Others will respect you for having the strength to look beyond yourself and consider the needs of others.

Interestingly, in a social capital community benchmark survey of 30,000 American households, it was learned that people who gave of their time or resources in the year 2000 were 43% more likely than non-givers to say that they were very happy with their lives. A whopping 42% of volunteers were overall happier in their lives than non-volunteers. Confronting feelings of apathy and malaise, the University of Michigan study of income dynamics showed that 34% of the people surveyed were less likely than non-givers to say that they felt so sad that nothing could cheer them up. Additionally, 68% of the sample group were less likely to have felt hopeless about their lives or circumstances.

From these statistics it is clear that giving back, maintaining a spirit of generosity, and working to improve the world around us brings prosperity, happiness and feelings of success. The feelings generated by volunteerism and donations therefore cannot be discounted and can be used as a tool for checking in on one's vision.

Chapter 12
Re-Evaluate Your Vision
Adapting to change

"No one can go back and make a brand new start,
anyone can start from now and make a brand new ending."

- Anonymous

As you grow and mature, you'll find that your vision of what you want to accomplish in life might change. It's worthwhile to take some time to re-evaluate your vision, especially at important turning points in your life. When you graduate, when you get married, when you have children, when you change jobs or when something unexpected happens in your life, it is important to take a step back, reflect on your initial vision and revise it to suit your present reality.

Your vision statement probably shouldn't change every week or month, but there are points in your life when your vision will evolve into something more specific. Ask yourself periodically and at relevant intervals if the model of your vision is still relevant given where you are that day.

Start by asking yourself if your original vision still motivates you. Has your life experience adjusted your attitude about what's important for your future? Sometimes you'll need to set your sights higher. Other times you'll want to fine-tune your vision to include new discoveries you've made about your strengths and the opportunities that might present themselves. Always strive for realistic alignment of your Vision and your Plan so that you can maintain the Right Attitude about your own life journey.

Let me share with you an example of how someone can re-evaluate their vision to meet their current needs and realization. I recently ran into a childhood friend who is in the field of public education. The last time he and I spoke a few years back, he was a vice-principal at one of the public schools in my area and well positioned to becoming principal soon. As I recently saw him, he was smiling, looked healthy, and was full of cheer. In fact, I can't recall ever seeing him look as well as he did that day. However, when I asked him about his job, he told me that he was teaching. I quickly replied, "I thought you were on track to becoming a principal in the school district. What happened?" He explained that he was a vice-principal and had the opportunity to become a principal, which he did for a short period of time. However, he came to an important realization about himself. He said to me, "I don't want to work all year round. To me success is having time to spend with my wife and kids. I like to go fishing and camping in the summers. I don't want to get home late every day. I decided that teaching was the best thing for me because it allows me to do the things that I like to do and I feel that I am having an impact with my students." My friend clearly came to a point where he realized that for him, success was about having more personal time to enjoy life. When I thought back to the days when we grew up together, I could see that his re-evaluated vision for his career and his life made complete sense for who he was and based on his personal interests. It was great to see a friend who found his path to success and was living it every day.

If you're faced with a life altering experience, take a little time to reflect on how your life has changed. There is always something to gain from reflecting on experiences, especially if they have drastically altered your sense of self. Allow yourself the space and the time to re-evaluate your vision to see if it still makes sense for what you're trying to achieve in your life.

Remember that there's no such thing as a bad vision, but also remember that it helps to be flexible and allow your vision to evolve as you grow and learn more about life. Following these elements of understanding will help you deal with challenges as well as opportunities in your life as you continue your quest for success.

CONCLUSION

Your success is now in your hands. With the Frazier Formula working for you, it should become clearer where and when to adjust yourself, your vision, your plan, or your attitude. Using the components offered in Unit II will make it possible to more fully integrate the Frazier Formula into your life and ultimately set you on a steady course towards success. Start with a clear vision that is exciting and motivational to you. Make the plan work for you – take time to craft it, plan it and sustain it through the right attitude. The Right Attitude not only includes looking at "the glass" half full instead of half empty, it also means allowing yourself to process those experiences that may cause others to quit, in a way that will help you be more effective in achieving your vision.

BIBLIOGRAPHY

Bailey, Simon T. *Simon Says... Dream: Live a Passionate Life.* Infinite Possibilities Publishing Group, Inc.: Altamonte Springs, FL, 2003.

Blanchard, Kenneth, PhD. and Spencer Johnson, M.D. *The One Minute Manager.* William Morrow and Company: New York, 1982.

- and Patricia and Drea Zigarmi, ed.D. *Leadership and the One Minute Manager.* William Morrow and Company: New York, 1985.

- and William Oncken, Jr. and Hal Burrows. *The One Minute Manager Meets the Monkey: Free Up Your Time and Deal with Priorities.* William Morrow and Company, New York, 1989.

-and Steve Gottry. *The On-Time, On-Target Manager: How a "Last Minute Manager" Conquered Procrastination.* William Morrow and Company: New York, 2004.

Bleier, Rocky. *Fighting Back.* Warner Books: New York, 1976.

Carson, Ben with Gregg Lewis. *The Big Picture: Getting Perspective on What's Really Important On Life*. Zondervan Publishing House: Grand Rapids, MI,1999.

Cobbs, Price M, M.D. *My American Life: From Race to Entitlement*. Atria Books: New York, 2005.

Collins, Jim. *Good to Great: Why Some Companies Make the Leap... and Others Don't*. Harper Business: New York, 2001.

Covey Leadership Center. *The Seven Habits of Highly Effective People*. Covey Leadership Center, 1986-1996.

Graham, Lawrence Otis. *Member of the Club: Reflections on Life in a Racially Polarized World*. Harper Perennial: New York, 1996.

Jeralds, Adonis "Sporty". *The Champion in You*. Xulan Press: Fairfax, VA, 2002.

Hill, Napoleon. *Think and Grow Rich*. Highroads Media: Arden, NC, 2001.

King, Coretta Scott. *The Words of Martin Luther King Jr.* Newmarket Press: New York, 1967.

Lee, Bruce. *The Bruce Lee Story.* Blackbelt Communications: 1989.

Loehr, Jim and Tony Schwartz. *The Power of Full Engagement: Managing Energy, Not Time, Is the Key to High Performance and Personal Renewal.* Free Press: New York, 2003.

Mandino, Og. *The Greatest Salesman in the World.* Bantam Books: New York, 1968.

Maxwell, John C. *Today Matters: 12 Practices to Guarantee Tomorrow's Success.* Warner Faith: New York, 2004.

Porter, Michael E. *Competitive Strategy: Techniques for Analyzing Industries and Competitors.* The Free Press: New York, 1980.

Price, Hugh. *Achievement Matters: Getting Your Child the Best Education Possible.* Dafina Books/Kensington Publishing Corp.: New York, 2002.

Smith, Will. *Just the Two of Us*. Scholastic Press: New York, 2001.

Steiner, George A. *Strategic Planning: What Every Manager Must Know: A Step By Step Guide*. Free Press: New York, 1979.

Strege, John. *Tiger: A Biography of Tiger Woods*. Broadway: New York, 1997.

Westen, Robin. *Oprah Winfrey: "I Don't Believe In Failure"*. *(African American Biography Library)*. Enslow Publishers: Berkeley Heights, NJ, 2005.

Woods, Earl. *Training a Tiger: A Father's Guide to Raising a Winner in Both Golf And Life*. Harper: New York, 1997.

The
Frazier
Formula
For Success™

$$S = V p A^r$$

For More Information Visit:

www.frazierformula.com

Author Bio

As President and CEO of the Hill House Association, *Evan S. Frazier* oversees one of Southwestern Pennsylvania's most important and comprehensive community service agencies. He is responsible for developing and implementing the organization's strategic vision, which includes managing a staff of over 100 employees, overseeing a multi-million dollar budget, and providing outreach to 60,000-70,000 clients per year in the Hill District and the Greater Pittsburgh region.

In a few short years, Mr. Frazier has successfully led the agency through a strategic planning process that has positioned the agency for financial and programmatic growth. This includes the expansion and repositioning of an affiliated entity, The Hill House Economic Development Corporation. Under his leadership, Hill House has received numerous honors including the Dominion Impact Award for Project Safe Summer, the 2005 United Way Outstanding Campaign Performance Award, and others.

Prior to his appointment to Hill House Association, Mr. Frazier held a variety of distinguished professional roles. They included: vice president (strategic planning and finance communications) at PNC Financial Services Group, senior vice president of the Manchester Bidwell Corporation, and director of community relations with Eat'n Park Restaurants.

In 1998, Evan Frazier was one of 17 individuals to be named a national "Luce Scholar". The honor, presented through the Henry Luce Foundation, enabled Mr. Frazier to experience Asia for a year working at Shangri-La Hotels and Resorts in

Singapore and Hong Kong. Mr. Frazier served as a "McGinnis Distinguished Lecturer" at Point Park College where he taught courses in international business and marketing for several years. And in 1990, Frazier co-founded the National Society of Minorities in Hospitality (NSMH), the nation's leading student-run organization for minorities in the hospitality field with chapters across the United States and the Caribbean.

An active member of the community, Mr. Frazier has served on more than 20 boards since graduating from college to include the Carnegie Museums of Pittsburgh, Carnegie Science Center, Greater Pittsburgh Nonprofit Partnership, Phipps Conservatory and Botanical Gardens, Pittsburgh Central Keystone Innovation Zone, Urban League of Greater Pittsburgh, West Penn Allegheny Health System, and YouthPlaces.

Mr. Frazier received his Master's degree from Carnegie Mellon University's H. John Heinz School of Public Policy and Management. He received his Bachelor of Science degree from Cornell University's School of Hotel Administration. He also completed a number of executive management certificates including Harvard Business School's Strategic Perspectives in Nonprofit Management, Program on Negotiation at Harvard Law School, and Boston College's Corporate Community Relations certificate.

Mr. Frazier is married to Holly Hatcher-Frazier and they have three children: Evan Jr., Nia, and William.

Infinite Possibilities Publishing Group, Inc.

Books and Media Catalog

Infinite Possibilities Publishing Group, LLC.

Office: 321-244-1329 | Fax: 321-244-1311

www.IPPublishingOnline.com - contact@ippublishingonline.com

Overcoming the World One Verse at a Time...